BUSINESS

TRENDS

KALEIDOSCOPE

BUSINESS

TRENDS

KALEIDOSCOPE

ROGER J. GOODMAN

KERNOW ENTERPRISES INC.
CALGARY, ALBERTA

First Edition, 1994

Credits:
Cover Illustration and Design: Janine Shore
Book Layout: Senefelder Services, Calgary, Alberta
Printed by McAra Printing Limited, Calgary, Alberta
Canadian Cataloguing in Publication Data

Goodman, Roger J. (Roger John), 1944 -
Business trends kaleidoscope

IBSN 0-9698313-0-7

1. Economic forecasting - Canada   2. Business forecasting - Canada   3. Canada - Economic policy - 1991-   4. Twenty-first century - Forecasts.
I Title

HC115.G535 1994   330.971 064   C94-900422-7

Dedicated to Nina - wife, friend and partner in all respects, plus our two wonderfully challenging and fiercely independent protegy, Tristan and Amanda Jayne.

ACKNOWLEDGEMENTS

The ideas in this book have evolved and crystallized over twenty-three years of residing in Canada. I am indebted to innumerable people who I have met over those years from virtually all segments of Canada's economy from Newfoundland to British Columbia.

Initially let me thank my first employer, Bondar Clegg and Company Limited of Ottawa for offering me that vital first job and above all for bringing me to Canada. In particular, my indebtedness to Bill Bondar and Fabian Forgeron, both of whom offered me abundant challenges and unparalleled experience. Bondar-Clegg was symbolic of the entrepreneurial spirit of small business in Canada, and nobody cherishes their ultimate success more than I.

This book grew out of a series of lectures and seminars, which were initially developed for the Faculty of Continuing Education at the University of Calgary. The enthusiastic response to my original course outline was instrumental in converting concept to reality. In particular, my thanks go to the then Dean of the Faculty of Continuing Education, Dr. Bruce Hamilton for his guidance and encouragement. Special thanks must also go to the thousands of course and seminar participants over the years - there is a little bit of each of you in this book. Your comments and challenging perspectives made me define more clearly the future trends of the Canadian economy.

One person stands out for stimulating my thoughts on trends and futurism and that is John Kettle of Toronto. To me, John is one of North America's foremost futurists. I am constantly amazed at John's ability to take almost any subject and develop some new blinding insights. John Kettle together with Marc Zwelling created the Intercorporate Futures Group - a motley group of like-minded, future-oriented and stimulating individuals, who meet four times annually to "brainstorm" the future. It has been a wonderful arena for the sharing of ideas and insights, as well as being the catalyst for my own thinking and ideas on the future. The usual disclaimer applies: I alone am solely responsible for the contents of the book.

Finally, my fondest appreciation goes to my eternal source of inspiration, and my reality check, my wife of 26 years, Nina. Not only my best friend and source of constant companionship, but a truly talented and intelligent lady. Behind the scenes Nina, has been a perfect complement to my preference for the limelight. Not only could she find time to coax this fiercely independent Cornish character, but she managed a hectic family schedule as well as embarking on her own baptism into the book-publishing world.

BUSINESS TRENDS
KALEIDOSCOPE

Contents:

Preface xi

Part I   **The Economic Reformation**

     1   Setting the Scene 3

Part II   **Agents Provocateurs**

     2   Technology - Hardware to Brainware 11
     3   Demographics - The Numbers Game 37
     4   Environment - The Greenswell 51

Part III   **New Horizons**

     5   Value Creation from Basic Resources 75
     6   Designing our Future 95
     7   Health - Changing for the Better? 107
     8   Travel - The Itinerant Consumer 115
     9   Education - The Greying of the Grey Cells 123
     10   Retail - The Age of Discernment 129
     11   Personal Services - Time Dearth 137

Part IV   **The Future Workplace**

     12   Organizational Change 143
     13   The Future Job Market 155

Appendix   **Job Trends in Canada** 167

PREFACE

The immediate origins of this book can be traced to the mid-1980s. At that time I began teaching a series of seminars and courses at the University of Calgary on future changes in the Canadian economy. Yet, the insights offered in these sessions were filtering through my mind from my earlier days working in many diverse areas and sectors of government and the complete spectrum of the private sector from small business to large corporations. From a breadth of experience working in, or dealing with many sectors of the Canadian economy, I began to frame a model of long-term change. In a sense the book's foundation is a detailed micro-view of the components of the Canadian economy. This is then aggregated to achieve a global perspective of change.

I had been thinking for some time that the conventional view of the Canadian economy was somehow not for real. It was a phantom belying its real self. The dismal science of economics and its practitioners had little to say about the real economy. They had retreated to the subterranean opaque world of econometrics. This murky abyss was characterized by convoluted mathematics, a devoid sense of reality and an unwavering success rate . . . of always being wrong. Beneath our obsession with business cycles there were fundamental changes taking place - a foundation of shifting sands - unbeknownst to most.

As I studied the Canadian economy of the mid-1980s, however, I became convinced that the economy was undergoing a fundamental restructuring. I recall the period of dramatic change and overhaul in British history - The Reformation - and in this book I will call it the economic reformation. Yet, in the mid-1980s everything was congealing very positively in Canada. We had emerged a little bruised and battered from the deep recession of 1982, but things were on the upswing. Corporations were optimistic (even profitable), consumers were in buoyant moods and, not to be left behind, governments jumped aboard with their drunken sailor act of spend, spend, spend! Times were good, until everything came gratingly to a halt in a mountain of corporate, consumer and government debt as we entered the new world of the 1990s. While my philosophy of radical economic reformation appeared heresy to most in the mid-1980s, it looks appreciably more respectable in today's turbulent economy. Many of my students and business seminar participants urged me to make the commitment and collect my thoughts and musings into a book. It took a while, but their persistence has been fulfilled. This book has been greatly enriched by their commentary, dialogue, discussion and debate.

I believe that one of the major banes of society today is the lack of clear, insightful communication. The art of communicating to a wide audience has been lost in obfuscation, jargon, acronyms and pseudo-intellectualism. Most of our leaders have become totally out of touch with the average person. My seminars have constantly catered to a broad spectrum of participants from the trades, small business owners to professionals in both the private and public sectors. Invariably, the feedback I received was favourable in terms of communicating complex issues in a clear and understandable manner. I hope that this book achieves the same goal in reaching the widest audience possible, from students concerned about jobs to the professional worried about downsizing to the business person musing about what the future holds.

My hope is that the book has the same impact on the reader as it has had on many of my seminar participants - a thought-provoking, provocative and perhaps insightful view of Canada's future. Hopefully, it will stimulate people to re-think how the future unfolds in terms of business directions, trends, business opportunities and the job market. The conclusions are not easy to accept; Canada is at its economic watershed. It is on that same slippery path traveled by New Zealand about three decades ago. Our standard of living as we know it is up for grabs, without fundamental change in economic direction.

Without the recognition and acceptance that the future structure of the Canadian economy is fundamentally different from the past, we are indeed already beyond our zenith. Natural resource extraction and basic processing are in retreat; the future is about unleashing our human, rather than natural resource potential. This means innovation, creativity, technological literacy and a willingness to compete in the true international arena, rather than solely with our next door neighbor. It is a world in need of bold visionaries - a resource severely lacking in Canada's corporate and government ranks today! It is a world of small rather than big business - business entrepreneurs rather than business bureaucrats. Our ability to recognize and adapt to change has not been good. We continue to seek privileges and protection for rear-view mirror industries of basic commodities such as wheat, oil, coal, wood pulp, and basic processed goods such as steel. We continue to pamper many of these declining industries with government grants, loan guarantees, loans and bail outs. Canada will be a richer place without its bail-outs of steel companies, obscene farm support programs, and financing of high cost uneconomic oil projects. This is a guaranteed recipe for long term decline. Instead, we need to embrace the new value added sectors, niche markets, marketing our natural resource and infrastructure expertise, high technology and sophisticated services. We need to recognize the miniaturization of business. The future is the entrepreneurial small firm or the big firms simulating miniaturization, not the big, bureaucratic Goliaths of the past. Anything less will leave us, relatively speaking, economically impoverished.

The challenges are immense, as we are not alone. As the newly-emerging industrialized countries, euphemistically called NICs, continue to feed on the basic industries of the developed world's economies, all major industrialized countries will be forced to move up market. We will not be alone in establishing our presence in the knowledge-intensive, value adding production of goods and services. The high-tech frontiers will be pushed back by all advanced nations. The competitive intensity of the new economy will be ferocious, compared with the easy dominance we achieved in the past in natural resources extraction and processing. Yet, staying where we are is not an option in the face of the NICs and a world of commodity gluts rather than shortfalls. The advantages of natural resources endowment is muted in a world of globalization and shrinking horizons. Japan in the last thirty years has clearly demonstrated not only that a country can survive, but prosper, on the importation of virtually all raw materials for industrialization. Natural resource endowment no longer provides Canada with any sustainable global competitive advantages.

Ironically, we do have all the fundamental economic infrastructure - transportation, logistics, education, telecommunications - to progress. To achieve this the visionaries and change merchants must be allowed to prosper at the expense of the reactionaries, die-hards and self serving and self-centered political weeds and corporate paper-pushers. But, can we make it happen?

This book, I believe, paints a different paradigm of Canada's future. It is predictive rather than prescriptive in nature. Let others more qualified and bolder than I offer the prescriptions needed to translate my dream of Canada into bold reality. It is a travesty that a country endowed with so much is producing so little! If we don't make the radical, bold steps to change in the 1990s, the twenty first century will certainly not belong to Canada.

PART I

THE ECONOMIC

REFORMATION

1

SETTING THE SCENE

The Business Cycle Blues

Our economy revolves around the short term. Tactics always reign supreme over strategies. Unless this changes, Canada will be irreversibly condemned to mediocrity. The politicians mind-horizon is limited to the next election. The large corporation is even worse, governed by the next quarter's earnings. This North American fanaticism with the short term is best illustrated by our paranoia with business cycles. Economists are grossly overpaid for their unwavering focus on predicting business cycles - invariably wrongly! Meanwhile, beneath this solidity of business cycle gyrations is a foundation of unnoticed restructuring - the economic reformation.

It amazes me that in a so-called free enterprise system, business cycles still cause undue consternation and surprise. It is hardly a novel observation that they invariably recur. Unfortunately, they do not occur with any regularity. This, in fact, is fortuitous for most economists, who spend their life guessing incorrectly the next downcycle and upcycle. The average business cycle in North America actually lasts four years - that is the good news! The bad news is that the cycle can vary from 2 to 9 years - not good for predictability, but wonderful for building complex models and black boxes with unfathomable mathematics.

So business cycles are a fact of life. They are of variable severity, unpredictable amplitudes, and invariably recurrent. Now let's get on with life and worry that underneath the fickle world of business cycles Rome is burning! Economic reformation is at work and undermining our ability to compete, to increase prosperity and to generate meaningful employment for our children. To recognize this is to act. To ignore this is to perish.

The last recession in the early 1990s was long and protracted rather than deep. The tragic part of the last recession, however, was not the temporary loss of economic growth, but the permanent scars of lost corporations. Together with the deep 1982 recession chunks of Canada's industrial heartland particularly in Ontario have been permanently dismembered.

The significance of business cycle downturns is that they are wake-up calls, which can, if enacted upon, preclude permanent restructuring. Too often, however, companies obtain a false sense of security from economic recovery and shelve the fundamental change required. Yet, each downturn in the business cycle exacts its toll on these corporations, until they become so fundamentally weakened that they finally succumb in the next recession. Such false hopes are evident today in many sectors of our basic processing and manufacturing industries. These companies have tenaciously pulled through the last recession and now tentatively grow during the current muted recovery. But, many will succumb in the next recession of the late-1990s, which will probably remove another chunk of our industrial core and more household names. Only those languishing companies with the foresight to change their production processes, products and/or marketing strategies will prosper longer term. Fortunately, there are many examples of companies that react positively to recessions and use them as catalysts for innovation. In fact, the ground-breaking work of Gerhard Mensch (1975) clearly demonstrates that clusters of innovation are invariably coincident with depressions and recessions. Presumably, this reiterates the old adage that necessity really is the mother of invention.

Changing Our Mental Map

There is little question that Canada has arrived at its enviable position in the world prosperity league - number three after the USA and Switzerland on a purchasing power parity, per capita income basis - propelled by its natural resource and related industries. It is clear, however, getting there and staying there, requires a mental transformation. Resources got us there, but they can't keep us there. We can only stay by exploiting the true potential and competitive leverage of the intellectual capital of our people and our high quality modern infrastructure. In this respect we are well endowed, but we are guilty of grossly abusing our endowment. The future economy is not about evolutionary change, but a quantum leap to a new paradigm - equivalent to moving from an agricultural to an industrialized economy. Only this time the shift is based on knowledge and value-added concepts, as well as continuous innovation.

We Are Not Alone

As Canadians, we have a propensity to internalize our problems. In reality, the challenges, though accentuated in Canada (and likewise in Australia) by our dependence on resource industries, are common to all advanced industrialized countries. We are all searching for the holy grail of more value adding, knowledge-intensive production of goods and services.

As more developing countries enter the new league of dynamos - the so called newly industrialized countries (NICs) - the basic industries in all advanced industrialized countries will be marginalized. Resource extraction and basic manufacturing requiring mostly semi-skilled labor will continue to migrate wholesale to the NICs. It is not difficult to see why - lower cost labour, new facilities with new technology and cheap financing, and lower social and environmental standards. This particularly applies to a lot of industries that form the foundation of Canada's economy like pulp production, iron ore, steel, grain, basic petrochemicals, crude oil, cement and automobiles. Even, the once mighty Japan, though late to this process, is now entering the early throes of economic reformation. The label made in Japan often means no more than assembled in Japan, with components actually made in Taiwan, Malaysia, South Korea, Indonesia and Thailand.

Nationalists equate this is to a sell out through free trade agreements. In fact, free trade agreements only institutionalize the irresistible changing dynamics and a nation's relative competitiveness in world trade. Resisting economic maturity and moving to a post-industrial society is as inevitable as gravity. Resource and basic manufacturing industries will continue to migrate to the newly industrialized countries in Asia and Latin America with or without free trade agreements. A free trade agreement with Mexico will merely give us advantages in selling our expertise for their future industrial development. At best, Mexico's development as an economic power is accelerated by a North American Free Trade Agreement (NAFTA), but even without it Mexico would grow rapidly. It is ironic that the opposition to NAFTA in Canada is lead by the unions and left wing politicians, who supposedly "care" so much for the developing world. I assume care in their case stops at self interest!

The advanced industrialized countries have reached a watershed in economic development. The life cycle hypothesis suggests that all these economies are reaching maturity in terms of economic growth. This means for many that successive years of 3-4 percent real economic growth is a phenomenon of the past. Long term economic growth, for all but the enlightened, will be nearer two per cent annually. There is no real model of a post-industrial nation or the "new economy," despite our attempts to illustrate with "model" countries such as Germany and Sweden. Economic restructuring in these countries will become as formidable a challenge or more so than in Canada. What we often neglect is that we do have a sophisticated and modern infrastructure for leverage into a modern post-industrial society. We are not disadvantaged by our inherent strengths of people and infrastructure, but only by inept and often self-serving leadership.

Where From Here

The Reformation is upon us and change is inevitable. If we are prepared to look forward to the emerging sectors instead of looking back to shore up the old, there is hope yet for an invigorated, but restructured future. Alas, we will not be alone as we attempt to move up the value and knowledge chain and time is of the essence. This process is, strangely, not new. J. A. Schumpeter, the renown Austrian economist, long ago in 1943 captured the essence of economic reformation in his marvelously insightful book *Capitalism, Socialism and Democracy*. In this book Schumpeter coined the lovely phrase "creative destruction."

Schumpeter's words were:

> *"Capitalism is by nature a form or method of economic change and not only never is but never can be stationary..... The fundamental impulse that sets and keeps the capitalist engine in motion comes from the new consumers' goods, the new methods of production or transportation, the new markets and the new forms of industrial organization that capitalist enterprises creates. This process of CREATIVE DESTRUCTION is the essential fact about capitalism."*

This book will trace several themes that will dictate our future direction. Our ability to catch the wave will determine our level of future prosperity. This book will first discuss the fundamental metamorphosis occurring in the Canadian economy - a world of Reformation. This is the new challenging paradigm driven by entrepreneurs, ideas, creativity, innovation and globalization. It is about value creation, knowledge intensity, design, quality, differentiation and individualized markets. Forget mass production, scale economies, mass marketing, and shoddy quality. The days of hewers of wood and drawers of water are purely for sentimental reflection. To understand the implications of these trends we need to recognize a fundamental shift in resources from natural to human. No longer do natural resources hold the key to our future, it is held in the knowledge, skills and inventiveness of our people.

The book will build upon this theme by looking at value creation from our basic resources, as well as value creation from the knowledge building blocks. The increasing role of services will be highlighted, both the "knowledge intensive" service engines as well as the "low-end" service engines. The implications of a polarized work environment will be discussed. Intertwined will also be trends in the new dominance of business miniaturization - the thriving of small, fleet-footed enterprises at the expense of the lead-footed leviathans.

The book will first review the economic drivers of change - the agents provocateurs of technology, demographics and the environment. Technology will be a major enabler of change. Fundamentally, we have ridden the hardware wave of automobiles, trains, planes, steel and chemicals. We are now on the rocket-rise of informative technologies. The weird business of "chips," photons, electrons, polymers, DNA and all those ephemeral esoterica - the new world of space age materials, microelectronics, telecommunications and biotechnology. No person will escape their pervasive influence and they will change our lives dramatically, in such diverse areas as health care, education delivery, jobs, the office, the factory, the home, and the leisure environment.

The numbers game will affect us all - the wonderful phenomenon of demographics and population structure. The unparalleled predictability and untold forecasting gems that spew forth business trends, business opportunities and job shifts. Stand back and all will be revealed!

Another driver of our new economy will be the movement of environmental sensitivities to mainstream thought; what I call the "Greenswell." Not to where radical greens want us to be, but certainly a marked shift in environmental consciousness. A shift to "pragmatic" environmentalism. The result - a myriad of business trends and notably new business opportunities and some major pitfalls for the reactionaries.

These major agents provocateurs will lead to new economic horizons, revamping many of the key sectors of our economy. Adding value to many of our basic resource and semi-processed products will be one of the major challenges as we move towards a more knowledge-intensive economy. Design will become a significant facilitator of change driven by changing tastes, aesthetics, technology, aging population, and environmental sensitivities. Design will become the embodiment of knowledge capture into the new products of the twenty first century. Adult re-training and education will be a critical component of this new knowledge-intensive economy. Population aging will ensure that health care remains front and centre although the funding and delivery of health care will undergo radical change. Other services such as tourism, retailing and personal services will also grow extensively, often in radically different ways than the past.

These will be the growth turbines of the twenty-first century and, by definition, provide "future" jobs rather than "retrospective" jobs.

The final section, therefore, will discuss what this means for the job market. In short, it will be a real metamorphosis, with a steady erosion of the comfortable middle - largely unionized, semi-skilled jobs. One of the peculiar long term dynamics will be the coexistence of persistently high levels of unemployment with skill shortages. Re-education and re-training will become a major challenge for the new Canadian economy. The dichotomy of high unemployment and skill shortages has major significance for Canadian society and forebodes increasing potential for polarization into "haves" and "have nots." Precluding this undesirable trend will require an understanding of, and reaction to, economic reformation within our economy. There is today little sign that our decision makers have the foresight or fortitude to change. Business as usual is the easier way to go, but with ominous implication for our society.

The Groundswell Of Reformation

Several futurists have depicted the emergence of a post-industrial society, the new economy and the information age. In an allegorical sense, I find a lot of the appeal in the active term reformation. The original Reformation was a religious movement started by Martin Luther. From a unidimensional world of Catholicism emerged a new religious paradigm of Protestantism. The initial disciples of this new religion were truly heretics of their day. Yet, their brand of religion flourished even in the face of the dominance of Catholicism in the Europe of their day.

There are close parallels with the economic parochialism of today. Our leaders despise the futurist ramblings about economic reformation, with its implications for the decline of industrial society towards a new paradigm of adding value and knowledge processing and emphasis on services rather than goods production. Yet, the heretics will prevail and with a bit of luck I won't be burned at the stake! The march of the newly industrialized countries (NICs) cannot be stopped. In fact, this front wave of advancing industrialized countries are being joined by other infants from the developing world. Following in the paths of South Korea, Taiwan, Hong Kong and Singapore are the infant NICs of Thailand, Indonesia and the Philippines, and perhaps most ominously of all, the giant nations of India and China. It is these countries that will assume the mantle of industrialization - sucking the resource and basic manufacturing sectors from the advanced industrialized nations despite a mighty gnashing of teeth, much kicking and screaming.

The issue is simple: if we want continued economic growth in the future, sectors other than resources and basic manufacturing must provide the fuel. Fortunately, some are already there, others need to be primed. The skills set of the new engines of growth, however, are radically different to the basic resource-intensive manufacturing sectors.

PART II

AGENTS PROVOCATEURS

2

TECHNOLOGY -
HARDWARE TO BRAINWARE

HARDWARE TO BRAINWARE

Technological developments will continue to propel change in our society. It will offer the liberation to a more sophisticated entrenchment of knowledge into value added production, products and services.

Technology, after all, is the embodiment of organized knowledge into the development of new products, processes or systems for practical and productive human applications. Yet, technology defies prediction. Technology both surprises us by the speed of development (computers) and on the other hand its slothful development (electric vehicles). Let's not kid ourselves that we can forecast the timing or scope of technological developments with any precision. Technology itself is human - a result of human ingenuity. It interacts with the social and cultural melée and is, ultimately, a carrier of human consciousness. It is this interaction, that, in part, makes technological forecasting such an unfulfilling and fruitless endeavor.

The difficulties of technological forecasting are also compounded by the process of technical invention, innovation and development itself. Technology progresses along both a revolutionary and evolutionary path. Forecasting the commercialization of technologies in an evolutionary environment can produce tolerably accurate results. Unfortunately, much of technological development emanates from discontinuities or quantum leaps in knowledge; the infamous technological breakthrough!

In general, therefore, technological development does not follow a linear path. Many observers have recognized that technology tends to occur in bursts, or overlapping waves. In 1957, Gerhard Mensch, a German economist published a classical analysis of technology change. In his analysis he identified clusters of technological innovation, often associated with periods during and after economic downturns. It is tempting to observe that under duress we do become more creative. As the old maxim goes "necessity is the mother of invention."

Pursuing our technological wave theory, it is instructive first to review historical technology development. The early technological waves of the 19th century were largely waves of basic infrastructure and fundamental infrastructure processes. They were the early forms of infrastructural transportation and transmission such as canals, railways, telegraph and telephones. Part and parcel of these forms of locomotion were key process developments to produce steam, iron, steel and textiles. The next wave of development, and one most of us have ridden and now take for granted, is the phase of material production of goods. This would include the now accepted basics of our society - automobiles, aircraft, gasoline, chemicals, pharmaceuticals and an array of electrical and electronic appliances and gadgetry. The wave we are now entering is radically different. It is based not on tangible products, but ephemeral knowledge-based technologies. In scientific terms it is the murky unknown depths of electrons, photons, deoxyribonucleic acid (DNA), complex chemical molecules and neutrons. They are the technologies now catalyzing change and forcing us into a brave new world of high technology, science fiction. It is the world of microelectronics, biotechnology, lasers, nuclear energy, telecom-munications, robotics, advanced materials and superconductivity. Hence, our evolution from the era of hardware to a new era of brainware (knowledge intensive) technologies. In turn, we can observe movement through a spectrum of time, with operational and processing tasks requiring less and less direct human input. From pre-industrial society of humans with stone and metal tools, we evolved to the early mechanized era of machines with operator. This was followed in the mature industrial era of mechanization with remote operator to today's emerging robotic era. The future presages even more direct detachment of people and machines through imbued expert systems and ultimately artificial intelligence (AI - not to be confused with artificial insemination!).

The Pace Of Technological Change Is Accelerating... Or Is It?

It is trite today to say that technological change is accelerating, but is it really? We tend to cherish and savour the dramatic successes, but conveniently neglect the technical sloths. It is obvious that developments in the semi-conductor chip have revolutionized society starting in the 1980s. How would we survive today without our fifteen drafts on a word processor, junk fax and our porta-potty electronic gadgets? Yet, in many areas, surprisingly little has changed.

It is instructive in looking forward to the next twenty years, to also look back at the last twenty years as a reference base. The ubiquitous automobile has seen little real change. It still has wheels, a gasoline engine and it doesn't fly (with teenagers excepted!). It is true that it is somewhat smaller in North America, today's cars also have computers (do you really notice unless one has to pay for a replacement?) and there has been a marginal (microscopic) increase in new advanced materials. But, apart from style, it is the same old spruced up beast! It is still fabricated largely from iron and steel, has an internal combustion engine, wheels with tires, and the braking, suspension and transmission systems are largely unchanged. We may well ask what fundamental changes have occurred in cars, aircraft, battery technology, power plants and building structures in the last 20 years. The answer is a lot on the periphery, but much less in fundamental terms.

Thus, the pace of technological change is a two-edged sword. We are amazed by technological breakthroughs, but conveniently forget the technological sloths... and there are many!

But the new technological wave is attaining its commercial zenith and many revolutionary changes may be imminently upon us. Technology zingers will come largely in the fields of advanced materials, microelectronics, telecommunications, biotechnology and certain electrotechnologies.

THE MATERIALS WAVE

Materials have defined our existence from the very dawning of civilization. They will continue to exert their influence. New materials offer the potential of a more environmentally benign society - a world of design for disassembly, miniaturization, lower emissions, demassification, conservation, better fuel efficiency and the potential of materials recovery and/or recycling. Materials are an integral component of the advances in information technology, especially the world of microchips and fibre optics. The breadth of potential materials conservation in some areas is mindboggling. For example, in terms of carrying capacity, one kilogram of a basic raw material such as sand (processed to fibre optics) has the same carrying capacity as 300 tonnes of copper telecommunications wire. A ratio of 1:300,000 - that's demassification!

The future drive will be to new exotic metal alloys, polymers, super-plastics, composites and advanced ceramics. All offer the potential of substantial materials conservation in the range of orders of magnitude. It opens up a world of increasing consumption, but decreasing materials intensity and use. Materials will remain fundamental to the evolution of civilization and will lead us to true post-industrial consciousness.

Materials Beings

The history of the development of materials science is, in reality, the history of civilization and society itself. Epochs of human development have been defined by the discovery and use of different materials. From the Stone Age we progressed through the Bronze Age and into the Iron Age. Nearer to our time we entered the Age of Steel, until today we are now into the new Age of Space Materials. The latter is the exotic science fiction world that gives us new polymers (or plastics), composites, velcro and advanced high temperature ceramics. From these we trespass into the translucent worlds of liquid crystal polymers and thin film diamond materials. New vistas of technologies are opened up by these new materials, including the semi-conductor itself, superconductive wires and the new information superhighways - the world of fibre optics. We are material(s) beings!

Price/Performance Ratio

The war is heating up, as a barrage of new materials encroach upon the domain of traditional materials. This is no longer a world of price alone, but the price/performance ratio. Consumers will pay for performance, even in the face of higher prices. Just take a look at the lowly tennis racket. Twenty years ago wood reigned supreme, but today it is almost impossible to buy a wooden racket. Rackets today are composite materials - carbon fibre, boron epoxy, and other composites. They certainly are not cheaper; in fact, they are much more expensive than wooden rackets. But the performance - ah! One can hit the ball faster, more accurately due to a large sweet spot, and the shock absorbency of composites, helps to alleviate stress injuries such as tennis elbow. Advantage performance!

The future will be more about price/performance ratios in materials than prices alone. On this basis expect a wave of new materials and a wave of new applications for polymers, composites, ceramics and metal composites. The brunt of this assault will be borne by the old industries of steel, glass, aluminum and paper, which are all at varying levels of maturity and even decline.

Plastic Invasion

Nothing competes with polymers for flexibility and versatility. This is hardly surprising given that there are today about forty different types of major building block plastics and perhaps over 10,000 specific plastics...and growing! The volume of plastics used in North America first exceeded steel in the late 1970s; the gap has been widening ever since. The future will see an acceleration in the drive and move to plastics.

Plastics have many characteristics in vogue in modern society. None are more important than light weight (this equals cost savings), aesthetics (color, texture), design, resistance to breakage and microwaveability. Plastics are about one fifth the weight of steel and half the weight of aluminum. In addition, specific plastics can demonstrate a host of other desirable characteristics - high strength, solvent resistance, high temperature resistance and high mechanical stress. Some of these features may come at a high price, but technology and reduced processing costs will bring many of these products to market over the next decade or so. Look at steel today, you will see plastics tomorrow.

Expect plastics to eventually dominate the packaging industry, despite ill-informed environmental opposition (for details see the chapter on "Greenswell"). Plastics out-perform glass in terms of light weight, versatility of shape and resistance to breakage. Metals are defeated on the grounds of light weight, versatility of shape and color and, significantly today, microwaveability. Expect dramatic growth in many engineering applications; for example, the body panels for a range of transportation equipment especially cars, buses and light rail transit systems. This will have a particularly devastating impact on the world's steel and aluminum industries. Bear in mind, that total world steel industry production in 1992 was virtually identical to 1973. One of the major reasons has been materials substitution. Yet, plastics still haven't reached into steel's big tonnage items in durable goods and construction members.

As technology advances, the last bastion for encroachment for plastics will be load-bearing structures. The plastics already exist, but costs remain prohibitive and the behavior of many plastics in fires remains a concern (both flammability and in some cases toxicity). Beyond the turn of the century, however, plastics in load-bearing structures will be making inroads, as alternative solutions to fireproofing are found (for example, fire-proof sheathing) and unit costs diminish with technology developments.

Many of the more advanced polymers and also the more expensive composite materials still command price premiums over steel. But, even today many polymers and composites may be cheaper than their steel counterparts when viewed in a total systems perspective. First, many aspects of performance may be superior - light weight, corrosion resistance and aesthetics. Light weight can mean transportation savings and corrosion resistance enhances durability and longevity (all are environmental pluses). Secondly, major cost savings may accrue in manufacturing and assembly through a large decrease in the number of parts. Thirdly, there may be a large reduction in tooling costs.

Plastics can be moulded to an infinite variety of shapes and a one piece plastic component can replace as many as forty to fifty separate steel pieces. The savings are multifarious - no fasteners, rapid fabrications (seconds versus hours for steel), pre-colored and no assembly. The result - substantial savings in assembly and manufacturing costs. In turn, large savings in tooling costs can also accrue. In general, tooling costs for polymers are 15-20 percent of the costs of metal presses. The days of polymer panels and super adhesives are close at hand. The world of the 1990s and beyond will evolve into a total systems cost where total component cost is equal to material cost plus assembly cost plus tooling cost. Plastics' advantages in this world begin to look unassailable and irresistable.

Composites - Better But Pricey

Composites have it all - strength, stiffness and light weight...at a price! These are true space age materials, first developed for the ultra-demanding environment of extra-terrestrial transport. These are the materials of space science fiction and high-tech world of spy activities. Their non-conductive and low dielectric properties render them transparent and undetectable to radar. But, these composites may be several times more expensive than aluminum and up to an order of magnitude more expensive than steel. Composites have the advantage of strength - they are essentially elongate fibres of various elements (carbon, graphite, boron, silica) in a polyester or epoxy resin matrix. It is the random directional properties of the fibres that give composites their large strength.

They are coming into their own in certain applications, mostly aerospace, automotive, electronics and consumer recreational products. Already the latest military aircraft often contain as much composite material as aluminum. By the year 2000 as much as 30 percent by weight of new, civilian planes will be composite materials. Reduced weight is a driver - for each one kilogram of weight reduction in a large jet aircraft, fuel savings can be around $2,000. This is becoming more, not less, important in the intensely competitive battle of the airways. Composites can also reduce fabrication time for aircraft, resulting in a reduction in fasteners and a possible reduction in tooling costs.

The next major battleground for composites will be the automotive sector, either as advanced polymers or composites. Non-price related issues will drive the materials game. Short product life cycles, aesthetics, durability, and fabrication and manufacturing flexibility will favor a shift from metals to polymers. The reduced number of fasteners and components and the development of super adhesives will accelerate the utilization of polymers and composites. A total system approach to automotive manufacturing will create the impetus for new materials. In turn, a growing desire for fuel efficiency without sacrificing size will lead to an inexorable increase of lighter, high-strength engineered plastics and composites.

Finally, composites, on the basis of their performance, will continue to invade the domain of the personal consumer. The leisure sports industry - rackets, fishing rods, baseball bats, golf clubs - is becoming dominated by composites. Expect the home environment to be the next frontal attack by the versatile composites, including kitchenware, cabinetry and cookware.

Ceramics - From Dinnerware To Industrial Components

Hot stuff - that is the world of advanced ceramics! Ceramics, themselves, are hardly new. The humble clay pot can be traced to the dawning of our civilization and through history has evolved to the ubiquitous ceramic tiles, fine china, potteryware and even the oft-used toilet bowl. Beyond these conventional ceramics, however, is a world of exotic high-tech, advanced industrial ceramics. These consist of two contrasting applications - electroceramics, the basis of our computing/electronics industry, and the structural ceramics focusing on broader industrial applications.

Advanced ceramics have many desirable properties such as high strength, wear resistance, high temperature resistance, hardness and light weight. Partially offsetting these advantages are their brittleness, potential for sudden failure, and difficulty of fabrication and machining. The raw materials for ceramics are cheap, but their processing and synthesis complex. Most advanced ceramics are metal or non-metal oxides such as zirconia, alumina, silica or non-oxides such as silicon carbide and silicon nitride. The manufacture of these ceramic powders is not for the backstreet powdered chemist - this is the world of frontier materials science such as solution - gelation, plasma synthesis and laser synthesis.

Electroceramics are already big business in the information technology world, as substrates for microchips, insulators, ink-jet printing, fibre optics and capacitors. The real future potential is for structural applications, that could revolutionize many facets of industry. This could vary from basic consumer products to tools and dies and ultimately to the all-ceramic automobile engine. Opportunities abound for both small and big business.

The basic consumer market is ripe for picking in the future. Basic cutting materials such as knives, scissors and snipping garden tools represent ideal markets. Advanced ceramics are more expensive than steel, but performance is no contest. The blades of ceramics will last 50 to 75 times longer than steel in many applications. Beyond simple consumer applications, ceramic blades will find increasing applications for cutting in paper mills, textile mills, carpet mills, steel mills and agricultural and domestic cutting machinery. A thin edging of advanced ceramics would prevent the wear on soles and heels of footwear - bad news for the shoe-repair business!

Advanced ceramics offer exciting potential in the medical field, due to their wear resistance and biological inertness. They are ideal for joint replacements, dental prosthetic devices and inert and non-toxic replacements for mercury dental fillings. In terms of both aesthetics and performance, ceramic braces will replace steel braces in dentistry. Ceramics offer the dental patients' dream - the barely visible brace!

Moving into industrial applications, advanced ceramics are beginning to replace steel in the tool and die industry and outperform metals in many heat exchanger applications. Many industrial components requiring wear resistance and exposure to high temperatures are ideal candidates for metal replacement by advanced ceramics. Some of these are already commercially viable such as turbochargers and hot glow plugs in diesel engines. Future emphasis will centre on increasing the number of ceramic components in automobile engines, with the ultimate objective of the all-ceramic automobile engine. The latter, however, on a commercial basis seems to be a glint in someone's eye. The Japanese car manufacturer, Isuzu has been working diligently for many years on the adiabatic ceramic internal combustion engine. The well-touted advantages of improved fuel economy, lightweight, and no cooling system still seem overridden by fabrication costs (near shape processing), lubrication problems and problems with microcrystalline cracking. Commercial realization still looks distant. The thrust, however, will turn much more to introducing a range of high performing ceramic components for the automobile, such as valve guides, pistons, pre-combustion chambers, turbocharger rotors and housings, port liners and water pump seals. Thus, ceramics will probably continue to contribute to the evolution of the automobile in terms of light weight, high performing components, lower fuel consumption, smaller cooling systems and maybe lower emissions (especially particulates).

BIOTECHNOLOGY - GENE PLAY

Biotechnology is in some respects a new face on an old technique. Some products of biotechnology take us back, yet again, to the dawning of civilization. Bread, wine, beer, cheese and yogurt have been around for centuries or even millenniums. Yeast was probably first used to make wine and beer as early as 6000 B.C. - that is what one calls a real vintage!

So what is biotechnology? It is simply the use of organisms and their cellular components to produce useful products, such as food, chemicals and medicine. Fermentation is a basic biotechnological process, as is composting. What is new is our understanding of the fundamental genetic structure of plants and organisms, which permits us to modify micro-organisms, plants and animals to produce specific characteristics, traits and properties. We finally have the ability to "play" with nature itself, with all its potential advantages as well as safety, ethical and moral concerns.

The ramifications of biotechnology are truly immense and will impact on all facets of society. Health care, agriculture, environmental cleanup, oil recovery, criminal detection and mineral processing could all be revolutionized to varying degrees.

Gene Factories

We are now entering the era of harnessing and manipulating genes for the benefit of humankind. At the core of modern biotechnology is DNA, or Deoxyribonucleic Acid, a natural component of all cellular material. DNA contains genes, which carry the various inheritable traits.

Genetic engineering or modification can change or insert different genetic coding into recipient cells. The benefits to biotechnology are in two major areas. The first enables us to isolate useful genes from plant and animal cells and transfer them to micro-organisms such as bacteria, which act as huge genetic manufacturing plants. The second allows us to transfer useful genes from one animal, plant or micro-organism to an unrelated species, which will incorporate the favourable genetic trait.

Obviously, this can create plants and animals with very different characteristics, hopefully desirable and beneficial traits, but not necessarily. Hence, the moral and ethical dilemma for biotechnology and the debate about what is, and what is not beneficial. The tampering with the very essence of life can undoubtedly have grave implications for societies, without comprehensive guidelines and regulations.

Genetic engineering has already started to deliver the goods. A range of commercial pharmaceutical products is already produced by genetically engineered micro-organisms. These include human insulin - now the most commonly used insulin by diabetics. The drugs include the human growth hormone to treat dwarfism, tissue plasminogen activator (TPA), a particularly effective drug for cardiac arrest victims and epidermal growth factor for treatment of burns and wounds. Many more have now been approved or are undergoing the testing and approval process. Beyond the turn of the century biotechnology may provide our best hope for developing anti-cancer drugs or an AIDS vaccine.

Animal Agriculture

Biotechnology is already favorably impacting the productivity and economics of livestock production. New vaccines are controlling diseases, hormones are increasing yields and embryo transfer and more advanced methods are producing livestock with enhanced favoured traits.

Infectious diseases take their toll on livestock in many forms. Livestock succumb to brucellosis, scours, gastrointestinal diseases and a variety of respiratory diseases. Many of the existing vaccines for the more common livestock diseases such as scours, influenza and bovine respiratory diseases are not very effective. New vaccines produced through genetic engineering are now appearing and have demonstrated enhanced efficiency. A further advantage is that many of these vaccines are cheaper to produce than through standard vaccine production methods.

Biotechnology will revolutionize the productivity of animal husbandry through upgrading of stock quality and incorporation of desirable characteristics. Artificial insemination and embryo transfer have already transformed livestock breeding from a chance event to a highly tuned, controlled scientific process. The result is the transmission of only the most desirable genetic characteristics from superior animals to multitudinous offspring. The impact - dairy cattle that produce more milk with higher butterfat content, leaner beef cattle and lean pork pigs.

The future potential is far greater. Semi-commercial operations already exist for livestock cloning - literally the exact replication of the most desirable traits from prized animals. Beyond is the even more sensitive world of "transgenics" and a world of mixed species. These animals carry certain advantageous genes transferred from other species.

New biotechnology products are being commercialized that will greatly increase yields from farm animals. The hormone, bovine somatotropin (BST), a naturally produced hormone in cattle, has been genetically engineered and used to enhance milk production and beef production in cattle. Cattle injected with BST can produce up to 25 percent more milk (they do eat more feed) and in beef cattle it can result in leaner meat and an enhanced weight gain of up to 15 percent. Similar techniques

---

SHOWCASE

Alta Genetics Inc., Calgary, Alberta

Alta Genetics Inc. is a sophisticated biotechnology company specializing in cattle breeding, using frontier embryo transplantation techniques. Based near Calgary, the company pioneered commercialization of embryo transfer in the early 1970s - a world first.

Alta Genetics high-tech breeding company has developed some of the premium dairy and beef breeding stock in the world. The company exports premium livestock worldwide as live dairy and beef cattle, frozen semen and frozen embryos.

The company is at the leading edge of biotechnology research, emphasizing cloning embryos by nuclear transplantation. Several hundred cloned pregnancies, all genetically identical have been successfully accomplished. Commercialization of cloning is imminent. The company is also embarking upon new research into transgenic livestock carrying genetic expressions for proteins, capable of yielding valuable drugs for human health.

The company was recently a finalist in the Canada Awards for Business Excellence in the invention category. This award was for Alta Genetics' development of a reliable non-destructive method of determining the sex of cattle embryos and applying DNA applications, enabling breeders to pre-select sex.

Alta Genetics is an example of the future....now! It is a high-tech niche, entrepreneurial business. It has high value-added, through intensive knowledge processing, and is a small business operating on a full global scale.

are now being used in sheep and pig production. The techniques remain controversial, however, and continue to meet opposition from biotechnology ethnicists, as well as farmers who fear either over-production (and hence lower prices for their farm products) or herd reduction to counterbalance increasing supply (in reality having a deleterious impact on the quota problem of the molly-coddled Canadian dairy farms). Here in a microcosm is the dilemma of biotechnology and the sensitivity surrounding genetic tampering. The gains in livestock quality and productivity are truly immense, but progress will be halting as the obstacle course of regulations, ethical concerns, and self-interest retard public acceptance. Directionally though, the march of biotechnological developments is unstoppable - disease resistance, new vaccines, more productive livestock and modified species will give a major boost to agricultural productivity and global food production. More for less will be offered by biotechnology breakthroughs.

Crop disasters have plagued humans from the days of earliest civilization. Famine and pestilence have been a constant reminder of our vulnerability to nature's darts. Crops succumb to bacterial and viral infection, the vagaries of weather, the plagues of insects or the pervasive throttling by weeds. We have tried to counteract many of these hazards through chemicals spraying to kill pests and weeds. As we now know, this has exacted a large cost on the environment, with chemicals such as DDT and dieldrin also destroying useful and essential elements of our biological and ecological systems.

Biotechnology promises a more positive, but potentially benign, solution to enhanced crop production. In the first instance, biotechnology permits more selective breeding programs, by allowing the transfer of only specific genetic traits. In addition, genetic engineering permits the incorporation of favorable genetic characteristics from unrelated species - the world of "transgenic" plants. The implications are significant in terms of reduced food costs, improved crop productivity and enhanced sustainable development through more effective use of chemical herbicides and pesticides.

The role of biotechnology in enhancing the world's production of food at lower cost and in helping to irradicate poverty and famine in the developing world is profound. Genetic manipulation permits the development of crops resistant to disease, pesticides and herbicides. Introduction of certain genetic traits would make crops more tolerant to environmental stress such as frost, wind, mould from excessive moisture, drought and salinity. Genetic engineering could result in higher yields, higher protein levels, varying oil characteristics (for example, lower saturated fats) as well as potentially self-fertilizing (nitrogenous fertilizers) cereal crops.

Future vistas are unlimited. Natural insecticides abound in nature - the isolation of these proteins can be made by genetic engineering and a representation of the gene can be inserted into a plant's genetic material. The plant is, thus, immune to attack by leaf-eating pests. Tomato plants with genetically enscribed natural insecticides are already commercial. Similar genetic transference has also been accomplished in tobacco for disease protection from the mosaic virus.

Herbicide use is coming under increasing scrutiny in a more environmentally-sensitive society. There is a strong motivation to develop environmentally-friendly herbicides, preferably with broad spectrum application. Glyphosate is one such environmentally-friendly herbicide, but unfortunately it tends to kill crops as well as

---

Agents Provocateurs

a wide range of weeds. Genetic engineering is now being used to breed crop plants resistant to glyphosate, hence permitting its use as a broad spectrum herbicide.

Environmental stress on crops is ubiquitous, often resulting in catastrophic crop failures with their accompanying human misery of famine, starvation and disease. Genetic manipulation will permit the development of stress tolerant crop species - tolerant to minor frosts, drought, salinity, excessive moisture and wind. In a Canadian context, substantial revenue is lost by farmers in late- summer due to an early frost in the Prairies. The result is subsequent degradation of wheat from high quality use in bread to lower value cattle feed. In such instances, biotechnology could, potentially, through development of frost-resistant strains, greatly enhance farm revenues.

Changing the inherent characteristics of many plants also opens up many avenues for increasing crop productivity and value. One of the early major successes of cross breeding in Canada was the successful modification of rapeseed to canola. The rapeseed plant yielded ample oil, which was toxic to humans. Successive breeding modification lead to the development of canola, yielding an edible oil and spawning a huge new cash crop industry for Canada. Today genetic engineering is being used to develop other crops as potential "oil factories." Much work has been carried out with flaxseed to develop modified varieties capable of high yields of edible oils with dietary acceptable characteristics (low saturated fats and lower cholesterol) or a range of specialty, customized oils. "Linola," from flaxseed, will become an important new cash crop for the Prairies. It will help displace imported cooking oils and provide an alternate raw material for oilseed crushers in western Canada.

Genetic engineering has the potential to revolutionize the agricultural industry with the development of novel commercial crop varieties. Genetic engineering accelerates the whole process of crop breeding and development of hybrids. Gene splicing can achieve, in a year, what conventional breeding achieves in five to eight years. Enormous savings can be garnered in selective pest eradication, without the harmful effects many pesticides now have on benign organisms.

Genetically improved varieties of canola, flaxseed, soybean, rice, alfalfa, tomatoes and other vegetables are likely in the 1990s. Genetic engineering may enable the production of specialty miniature soybean on the Prairies. This is used in Japan to make natto and these soybeans command a premium price.

Rapid progress is also being made in genetic engineering of cereal crops. Genetic modification of cereal crops, or dicotylids, has continued to defy the scientists, until recently. Now we appear to be on the verge of a breakthrough, by the recent introduction of foreign genes into wheat. This could lead to the development of "designer" cereals and cereals with the characteristics of legumes in terms of nitrogeneous self-fertilization.

Genetic Food?

Beyond genetic engineering of basic crops, the next decade is expected to lead to biotechnological breakthroughs in food processing. This is one of the major opportunities in Canada for the development of a true value-adding agri-business. Biotechnological developments will result in fruit and vegetables retaining their freshness longer, improved texture, improved flavour, better nutritional content, enhanced preservation and the development of superior food additives. A major product of biotechnology is enzymes, which will play a much bigger role in the food processing industry of the future. Enzymes not only can carry out very complex chemical reactions, but have the ability of very high customization of products. They are the very model of the new economy of individualized production.

Biotechnology will ultimately lead us to the world of broad-based agricultural factories, where a basic cereal feedstock may be the basis of a complex biotechnology processing plant that produces starch, proteins, alcohol, animal feed, fibre and even an array of pharmaceuticals. This would be the long-sought after agro-industry - the true fusion of agriculture and industry through the enabling characteristics of biotechnology.

The Human Side

Modern biotechnology is opening up a new spectrum of possibilities in the detection and treatment of human disease. Commercial success is already evident and will likely accelerate in the 1990s, as the laborious work of the 1980s research and developments bears fruit. The red ink that plagued many biotechnology venture capitalists in the 1980s will run to the black ink of profits in the 1990s.

Diagnostics offers the greatest reward. DNA categorization will provide new opportunities for early and timely diagnosis of certain diseases. Even today few diseases are untreatable if early detection is achieved. Monoclonal antibodies, in particular, are molecules that specifically attack a given virus or bacteria. This attribute will be used to advantage in biotechnological development. Such techniques will lead to a large growth in the home test-kit market for a wide range of diseases such as AIDS, specific cancers, sexually transmitted diseases and various immune deficiency diseases. Gene- or DNA- probes are also being developed as primary diagnostic tools. Gene-probes, through chemical labeling of specific parts of the DNA can, in addition to identifying existing diseases, also assess the potential for disease or genetic defect. Gene-probes are being used to test foetuses for Down's syndrome, sickle cell anemia, hemophilia and muscular dystrophy. There are now over thirty diseases that can be diagnosed by molecular techiques. On-going research is shedding light on specific genes responsible for, or with a predisposition towards certain diseases. This will enable proactive treatment to be administered to thwart or ward off the onset of diseases in many instances.

Gene Snoops

The use of gene probes is now expanding beyond the boundaries of medical diagnostics into individual recognition techniques for forensic and criminal investigations. No two individuals possess the same genetic composition. This is now being used by forensic scientists to identify individuals from any traces of blood or tissue remaining at the site. DNA finger printing is becoming part of the forensic lexicon and is being used increasingly to provide evidence in paternity suits, rape cases and other violent crimes. Further uses will be in the provision of evidence against hunters of endangered species or hunting within the national parks. The advantages of DNA genotyping is that it can be conducted on any human tissue fresh or dried, including hair, blood, semen or skin.

Genetic Drugs - The Coming Tide

It is in the field of drug production that biotechnology developments are becoming more evident. Biotechnology offers several advantages to conventional pharmaceutical production:

1. potential cost savings in manufacturing;
2. synthetic production of rare substances;
3. human gene derivatives should have fewer side effects than animal derived products (for example, insulin) and the synthetic product is often of higher purity;
4. synthetic production is unconstrained compared with natural derivatives (for example, insulin).

It is not surprising, therefore, that many companies are pursuing drug production via genetic engineering processes. Biotechnology companies have targeted almost every human disease and keep discovering hormones, proteins and enzymes with unique properties to counteract diseases. Still the human therapeutics industry, though the largest branch of commercial biotechnology, is still a small industry. Just over a dozen biotech drugs have been commercialized, with another couple of dozen are now progressing through the laborious and slow multi-stage clinical trials in the U.S.A. Most of these new prospects for at least the 1990s fall into about seven major therapeutic categories:

1. colony-stimulating factors (CSFs) - to counteract infection and immune deficiencies;

2. monocolonal antibodies - used to attack cancer cells, toxins and viruses or used to deliver drugs/radioisotopes to specific hosts;
3. interferons - used to counteract infectious diseases and cancer;
4. interleukins - used in cancer therapy, wound healing and immune deficiencies;
5. growth factors - used in wound healing, damaged tissue regeneration and growth disorders;
6. blood factors - used in blood clotting;
7. erythropoietin - used to treat anemia.

It is important to recognize that the pace of biotechnological developments in the human therapeutic area is slow. Final approval of new genetically engineered drugs follows several lengthy stages of review, testing and clinical trials. This entire approval process averages 6-10 years, although a fast track process is being implemented to try to reduce the period of approval to an average of five years. Pressures for acceleration in approvals will become severe for many terminal cases of cancer and AIDS.

Biotechnology Processing For The 21st Century

The emphasis of biotechnology in the 1990s and beyond will remain with human health and agriculture. Beyond these, however, biotechnological processing will likely affect an array of other industries. Applications will develop in food processing, waste management, oil recovery, alcohol from biomass and in metals and minerals processing.

Biotechnology will play an increasing role in waste management. Human waste in sewage processing plants is already handled by biotechnology. Microbial degradation of human waste will be extended into other areas of waste management. They will be used to break down oil wastes, breakup oil slicks and treat pesticide, herbicide and other chemical wastes.

Cheap renewable fuels to replace non-renewable oil, gas and coal remain elusive goals for society. Current processes of producing alcohol fuels from biomass are very expensive, and invariably energy intensive. Ultimately, genetic engineering techniques must be developed if the vision of endless cheap, non-renewable energy is to be achieved.

Oil recovery remains an elusive challenge for biotechnology. The prize is large! Most depleted and abandoned oil wells in North America have only recovered 25 to 40 percent of the actual oil in place. Genetically engineered microbes provide the best potential solution for coaxing fine oil globules from their porous hosts. Various techniques are undergoing experimentation including in-situ production of biopolymers and the in-situ breakdown of viscous bitumen and heavy oil to light, pumpable crude oils. Microbes could also be used to induce fractures in oil bearing strata - rock digesting microbes, which would permit enhanced oil flow. Ultimately, the bio-processing of known oil deposits near existing infrastructure will become cheaper than moving to ever more distant and expensive exploration and development of prospective frontier oil reserves in North America.

Microbial recovery of metals has already been exploited in a small way, largely in the recovery of copper from mine tailings. The current recovery processes are slow, however, and small in scope. Genetic engineering could have a large impact on processing productivity, by increasing an organism's metal leaching and aggregating potential. In addition to pure altruistic metals recovery, the processes would offer excellent potential in environmental cleanup of hazardous mine tailings ponds, often abandoned by mine closures. Present mine waste could become the mines of the future.

Social Rifts

The technologies discussed so far - advanced materials and biotechnology - have changed society but information technology (IT) arguably has revolutionized society. Few of us have been untouched by the tentacles of information technology. The work environment, whether it be factories, mines, oil wells, offices, warehouses, schools, hospitals or stores, has been changed for ever. Computers, fax machines, telephone answering machines, E-mail, robotics, expert systems and automated teller machines have all become part of our daily lexicon. The home environment has been far from unscathed with microwave ovens, VCRs, CDs, wireless phones and, increasingly, computers and fax machines. In all respects, we have gorged on "chips." The microchip has revolutionized our life. While the economic consequences are well understood, we probably underestimate its impact on society, lifestyles and social interactions. The microchip is far from benign in its impact in these areas and has probably already torn at the social fabric of society. Let's look at some simple examples.

The compact disc is the first recording medium to deliver near perfect music. Free of distortion, hisses and cracks it provides the best of a near perfect listening experience. Why go to a live concert to listen to an unpredictable performance accompanied by coughing, crackling candy wrappers and impromptu, unsolicited and unwanted commentary from your audience neighbors? The world of VCRs delivers programming and movies on demand, at your convenience and low cost. Why bother going to the movies to pay high prices for tickets and concessionaries, stand in line, and end up with a high babysitting bill? Even the humble microwave has an underrated impact. It now gives us the propensity of quick food at our leisure. It alone has contributed substantially to the demise of the family meal. Rather than eat prescribed adult fodder, the kids can quickly concoct their own "nuked" food. Even the new technologies of fax and E-mail detract from the personal interaction of a telephone. A more detached, impersonal anti-social society is the outcome. This in many ways is the "cocooning world" of Faith Popcorn. The notion that we can enjoy all the experiences for which we formerly had to leave the home, now in the home itself. The home has become the perfect couch potato's home entertainment center.

As we have seen elsewhere, however, the real world is one of individualization and niche markets. In that respect Popcorn's view of the world has turned out to be less global in reality, although demographics has been on her side (the baby-boomers have been at peak family creation stage). For all the developments of in-home sports, movies, concerts and entertainment at our finger tips, people have not lost the urge for outside entertainment. The world of movie theatres has not gone into total decay, but has found a favorable large niche among people who want the real experience of a movie theatre, the big screen and the popcorn. Similarly, there is still nothing quite like the spontaneity and unpredictability of live concerts and theatre and the live rapport with the entertainers. But, no doubt information technology has revolutionized consumer choice and the home has become an extended entertainment centre. As in other facets of the economy, fragmentation is the wave of the future - in this case fragmentation of preferences.

Harvesting the Fruits

The Information Technology era is far from over. Indeed the 1980s may be the decade in which IT flowered, but the fruits have yet to be harvested. In many respects the 1980s laid the foundation of IT and put in place the infrastructure. But, it was disjointed, it was fragmented. It was a world of two solitudes - the microelectronic world of computers and the world of telecommunications. It was a world full of systems that could not communicate - software that did not match hardware, the non-communication of the electronic medium with digital medium and the constant leap-frogging of sub-technologies.

Already the IT revolution is maturing through the synergistic marriage of microelectronics and telecommunications into a unified digital system. This will enable users to maximize the potential of IT in terms of user-friendly, customer focus applications.

Dramatic improvements in IT are largely credited to the massive developmental leaps in chip technology. Yet, it is the total system that has advanced. Chip technology has permitted immeasurably faster processing and transmission. The IT infrastructure advances, however, are more than chips - they are the quantum leaps in computer architecture, software, storage technology and capacity and retrieval speed. More convenient input devices such as the mouse and touch screens, in conjunction with the development of ink-jet and laser printers have propelled acceptability. Voice-activated systems will catalyse receptivity even more.

In turn, the world of telecommunications has been turned upside down. The last decade has seen the development of digital switching, packet switching and statistical multiplexers. Fibre optics has become prevalent, resulting in low costs and a vast increase in transmission capacity and speed. Satellites, microwave and cellular telephones now permit widespread mobile and remote communications.

The combination of microelectronics and telecommunications to form IT has resulted in a proliferation of a new world of work including computer assisted design (CAD), computer assisted manufacturing (CAM), fax, E-mail, electronic data interchange, robotics, teleconferencing and expert systems.

Bridging Work And Home - The Portable Office

Technology is no benign agent of change. It reaches behind the self evident impacts into changes in lifestyle and culture itself. It has the stealth of a cat.

Information technology in the 1990s will start to blur our views of different facets of our existence. The clear definition of work and leisure will become a single blurred solitude. The new world of portability will bring the office into the home, the home into the office, the office into our leisure activities and even the factory into our home. A forbidding thought indeed! Imagine yourself transported by float plane to a remote lodge in the Yukon for some relaxing lake fishing, accompanied by your cellular phone, porta-fax and pen-based palm-top computer! There will be no escape through distance anymore! What the fibre optic world doesn't reach the world of satellites, microwave, digital and cellular will...anywhere!

In recent times we have evolved from a wired world to the start of a wireless world. Cellular telephones have penetrated the market probably faster than most people thought, in both the home and car environment. The next generation of cellular will be clearer, impervious to extraneous noise, and have extended distance range. Strangely their role in the office has been more muted, with good reason. Most modern office buildings have metal coated glass, which reflects not only harmful radiation from the sun, but also blocks cellular radio waves. Worry not, necessity is the mother of invention! Arising from this constraint is the next new technology - the world of digital cordless with its Darth Vader penetration of metal coated glass or the specific set-up of internal cellular receptor stations.

As with most technologies, wired phones, cellular and digital cordless complement one another, rather than displace each other. They will co-exist as a comprehensive network that will be integrated into a complete system for instantaneous contact, where incoming calls will search automatically all three applications and trace the recipient at home, in the office or factory or in their transportation conveyance (car or aircraft).

Telecommunications in all guises - phone, fax, conferencing - will be available from anywhere. Integrated into these applications will be the world of computers, with increasing emphasis on miniaturization and portability. Already represented in a primitive way as pocket organizers, they will blossom into full fledged notebooks and palm-top computers, using pen-based systems for input, only to be succeeded rapidly by their superior voice-activated relatives.

We are nearing commercial reality of pocket-sized computers, but with their miniscule difficult-to-use keyboard it will be finicky to use compared to their larger notebook cousins. Their success probably hinges on continuing commercial development of pen-based systems, or the rapidly advancing speech recognition technology (SRT). Emerging from the laboratory is a new array of commercial speech recognition products, with widespread application guaranteed by century's-end. This will be the ultimate "user-friendly" technology for computer hacks - no more "hunt and peck" or carpal tunnel syndrome. SRT already exists for vocabularies up to 100,000 words. The system is far from perfect, with speech speed still restricted to about 40-50 words a minute, compared with normal speech patterns of 150-180 words a minute. There is also a substantial "machine training" period of 15-25 hours to produce an effective voice recognition model. But, current systems are used very effectively commercially, especially for shorter notes or reports with somewhat constrained variability. Evolution of SRT from basic effectiveness to advanced capability is expected over the next few years. As this happens, both keyboards and pen-based systems will become basically obsolete.

Voice-activated computers will accelerate the acceptance of computers in the home and will revolutionize the mobile environment. Small computers absent of cumbersome micro-keyboards or inconvenient pen-pads will be a boon to mobility and the concept of computer accessability everywhere (even waterproof systems for the shower!). Voice technology will not be limited to the world of mobile computers, but will be used to activate and instruct automated teller machines, issuing verbal instructions for a range of applications and machines, and even the translation into foreign languages. The latter will be a major advance in a world of increasing globalization.

Multimedia - Hype or Reality?

The 1980s for the first time delivered us a hotchpotch of new information technologies and different media, with limited interconnectivity. Analogue technology co-existed (uncomfortably) alongside new digital streams. Computers revolutionized the workplace, and to a much lesser extent the home, but primarily focused on text, graphics and data. This coexisted with the telephone, which in the early-1980s was primarily for the voice medium. Fibre optics and the world of digital changed this two-part world of computers and telecommunications for ever. The two solitudes began to converge into a more integrated service.

Multimedia is the 1990s term or vision for conjugal integration of all media - data, text, graphics, voice, music and other media miscellany - into a fused digital whole. This opens up a whole new paradigm of competition in the information technology and media industries. This will undoubtedly be one of the economic battlegrounds of the 1990s, as competing infotech and media giants stake out their positions. This will pit cable companies against telephone companies against computer and software developers. The prize is immense - domination of the new mega- business of multimedia, likely to reign supreme in the first couple of decades of the next century. A plethora of new products and services will be offered to consumers. As a gynacologist would say, it is all in the delivery!

The winner of the delivery stakes take all - a multi-billion dollar industry, likely to become one of the largest growth industries over the next decade or so.

Digital Autobahns

The full integration of the telecommunication and computer industries now lies at the core of development of a fully integrated information society. These new intelligent networks or distributed computing systems will be unified into a digital whole. Digitalization simply means that the conveyance enabler occurs in the digital language of computers, rather than the waves or analogue form of today's telephones and televisions. Today, analogue is to digital, as vacuum tubes were to silicon chips.

High speed digital is the revolutionizing technology, enabler of the future. It will facilitate the new world of multimedia. Digital will provide the autobahns for all forms of media dissemination, all down the same fibre optic cable or via new powerful satellites. Copper wires will be the new dodo birds, exterminated by a technology orders of magnitude more efficient. When it comes to communications bandwidth, optical fibres are light years ahead. Our whole telecommunications circuitry is designed for the small bandwidth human voice, communicating at a tortoise-pace of 50-60 bits per second. Computers operate on a huge bandwidth for microsecond bursts. Using digital autobahns communications can occur at a staggering rate of over 100 million bits per second.

The world of digital is unstoppable - it is the ultimate information densifier. Digital video signals can be compressed such that vast quantities of information can be carried in fibre optics cables or satellite transponders. The new satellites boosting 120-watt transmitters will be an order of magnitude more powerful than existing 15-30-watt transmitters. Gone will be the giant and unsightly 96-inch satellite dishes of today, pushed aside by their sleek 18-inch or smaller protegy.

The digital battle of the next decade will be between the direct broadcast satellite(DBS) companies and the cable companies. Both are geared up to providing 500 plus television channels by the turn of the century. Unfortunately, the outcome will be determined less by technology and more by regulation. The Canadian Radio-television and Telecommunications Commission (CRTC) will no doubt flex its steroid-laden muscles as dictator, arbiter and filter to us consumers unfit to responsibly decide our own media consumption (woe betide we may go global with foreign content!).

Agents Provocateurs

Digital Evolution or Revolution?

The outstanding question for digital over the next decade will be one of gradual evolution or the quantum leap revolution. Vested interests, large investment costs and market-inhibiting regulatory constraints will probably favour creeping incrementalism. The bold quantum leap would entail a fundamental recognition that "tele" means dead. Both the telephone and the television are now anachronistic artifacts, already destined to the scrap-heap or museum for antiquities. There is simply no role for analogue technology in a world of digital. The quantum leap would exorcise any analogue-based system and make the revolutionary leap to massive interconnected and communicative computer networks. Telecomputers will ultimately be the universal digital medium conveyed by cable and by satellite. They will be mobile, office-based, home-based and factory-based. The digital cellular computer with speech recognition systems will sweep aside today's narrowly-defined cellular telephone. In turn, telecomputers will offer us the ultimate in entertainment - not 500 channels of duplicated programming, but access to unlimited personalized entertainment, imitating the choice we have in the printed media today.

The above is the brave new world of the quantum leap. We will no doubt get there eventually (2010?), but the more likely path is incremental digital. Telephone companies with a somewhat vested interest in survival will patch up their existing copper wire systems, boosting capacity through asymmetrical digital subscriber loop (ADSL) technology. Television companies will persevere with high definition television due to the enormous investments to date. Cable and direct broadcast satellite companies will release their barrage of choice with 500-1000 channel television, albeit the same inventory of programming packaged in 500-1000 different ways. The new television will offer neither real choice nor high definition (as the inferior American system of fewer lines will be retained). But, the key will be about politics and protected markets, not delivering what the customer really wants - real individualized choice!

Societal Implications of Digital

The new world of portability and blurring of home, work, and leisure solitudes is a catalyst for embracing the brave new world of digital. The home now assumes a fresh dimension - an epicentre for new telecommunications-based activities and services. Seven areas look poised for rapid growth and, by definition, an array of business opportunities over the next decade or so.

1. Home-Based Businesses

Combine digital with business minitiaturization and it is a sure bet that home-based business will flourish. The "burbs" will become the new business hubs. Communication will hardly be a problem as the home-becomes a denizen of high-tech wizardry of photocopiers, computers, modems, fax machines, videoconferencing machines and even electronic data interchange. The implications of this trend are more far-ranging than most people appreciate. First of all it creates a whole suite of new business opportunities for home-designed office furniture, integrated furniture concepts (for joint office-bedroom functions), electronic hardware sales, specialized home-based electronic hardware (smaller-scale and lower cost) and restricted space design. Even the clothing industry will be impacted, as home-based business leads to less formal and more informal wear.

Particularly unnoticed will be the substantial erosion of the income-tax base for all levels of government, as previously salaried employees become independent businesses. A salaried employee will generally pay more income tax than an incorporated small business. Home-based business will be a major challenge for local taxation authorities, as not only do they represent non-taxation revenue entities, but the flight from the traditional downtown locations will erode local municipal tax revenues. A double tax whammy!

2. Telecommuting

Long-hailed, its time has now come. Contrary to the perceptions of the "stuffed shirt" reactionaries, telecommuting represents a major opportunity for cost savings and productivity gains. Electronic contact with the office obviates the need for physical presence in many office environments. The most pervasive development will be the half-time telecommuter - half the time in the office and half the time at home. The benefits are obvious - less time spent in tiring commuting, a sharing of office space and the reduction in time consuming, unfocused meetings (the bane of modern organizations). Implications of telecommuting are indeed revolutionary. It involves first of all real trust between management and workers and true empowerment of employees. It has negative implications for conventional office space, especially in urban centres, where office sharing will become the norm and exacerbate the already looming surpluses of downtown office pinnacles (the last bastion of sub-conscious reflection of male egos!).

This, in turn, will lead to a major growth industry - refurbishing downtown office space to inner city housing. This will be focused especially in the up-market apartments and loft-type dwellings for the growing demographic wave of single persons and childless couples. Telecommuting, of course, will be a boom for the sales of electronic hardware. In the 1990s, the home environment will become the major catalyst for electronic computer and related telecommunications equipment sales.

3. Entertainment

Home entertainment in an advanced infotech era will become more customized and individualized. Initially, this will occur through conventional television with just a lot more channels. In many respects, this will be more of the same with much replication as well as regionalization of sporting events in the name of diversity. Beyond the narrow paradigm of more channels, however, we will evolve to the true telecomputers, capable of real individualization and choice of programming. Opportunities will abound for the creation of specialized and niche programs on virtually any subject, spurning a new industry of specialized electronic programming. The home will evolve to a multimedia entertainment centre, highly personalized to the individual. Contrary to many perceptions, however, this will not lead to the demise of live entertainment and outside-of-the-home entertainment. The arts, in general, will flourish as technology opens up new vistas and creative experiences. Virtual reality may become part of the living room experience within ten years, but the spectacular developments will be commercial utilization outside of the home, in theatres, advanced movie concepts (AMCs) and concert halls.

4. The Intelligent Home

An integrated home management system will be part of the new high-tech home. The evolution to home entertainment systems will allow full integration of home automation to control a host of appliances, heating, cooling and security systems. These will be introduced first of all in new homes, followed by retrofitting in existing home, as computers become the nerve centre of future residences. Health delivery programs will eventually be integrated into the intelligent home.

5. Remote Transactions.

Telecomputers will open up avenues for a large array of remote transactions. lead by telebanking and teleshopping. This will be driven largely by convenience and time saving. No more line-ups at banks and stores and a complete choice of time. Access to stores' inventories and pricing regimes from a home computer will intensify competition and lead to more competitive pricing for consumers. Telebanks will be more than accessing your accounts - they will become vehicles for ticket acquisitions, reservation services and a host of other services.

6. Personal Communications.

To date, personal communications have been virtually untouched by the age of information technology. With the proliferation of home computers and modems (and their future high speed derivatives) communication will get personal. Driven by speed and low cost, compared with a conventional mail system, personal communication will start with simple faxing of letters. This will soon evolve into a multi-faceted wave of personal communication involving text and images (including family and personal photographs which, of course, will be digitized rather than imprinted on chemical film).

7. Home-Based Education

As discussed in a later section, adult education will be a boom industry over the next decade. driven by both vocational needs and personal development and self-fulfillment. As part of home-based entertainment, more education will occur in the home. It seems inevitable that Canada will develop a more entrenched "open university of the airways" system. Supplementary education systems will be developed for children, focusing on designated school curricula. These will be spearheaded by selecting the country's true super teachers or communicators for country-wide electronic dispersion to compensate for the shortcomings of the conventional school and college systems, which steadfastly refuse to address the issue of poor teaching performance.

In addition, home-based telecommunications will greatly enhance the capability of students interacting with external information sources. New links will be established with libraries and other information and data bases to allow unparalleled access to information.

3

DEMOGRAPHICS -
THE NUMBERS GAME

Setting the Scene

In a formal sense, demographics is about human population, all aspects of human population. It is about people and what Roger Sauvé, in his recent book (Canadian People Patterns), calls people patterns. Reduced to its basics, however, it is a numbers game, pure and simple. It describes age profiles, gender, the workplace, households, immigration, labour force, births and of course, unfortunately, mortality, as well as a host of other aspects of population minutiae.

What makes it attractive is its predictability, due to the replication of general set patterns to our lives. Barring catastrophes such as famine, pestilence or epidemics, we can predict many facets of the future structure of Canada's population with amazing accuracy, even three to four decades into the future. Demographics gives us x-ray vision of the future.

Many quasi-demographic terms have been enlisted into the popularized vernacular - the greying of society, the age wave, the baby-boomers (and lets not forget their "echo"), the baby-busters, and the colouring of Canada. Many more terms are acronyms, which have drifted into common use - woopies (well off, older people), the somewhat less flattering woofs (well off, older farts), dinks (dual income, no kids), swanks (single women and no kids), spokes (spoiled kids of the eighties) and swakip (single women and kids in poverty).

Population structure has an important bearing on Canadian society. We are, among most industrialized societies, a young country, with young people, but from herein our population will be aging...rapidly. This statement is unequivocal and it alone will revolutionize the economic and social fabric of Canada. It will have far reaching ramifications on health care, pensions, education, organization structures, business employment and immigration policies. Few subjects are as important as demographics in terms of business trends and opportunities. Yet, none is more predictable.

A Checkered Past!

If, in fact, Canada's population growth, fertility rates and immigration levels and other factors had been constant over the past several decades, demographics would be rather tedious and uninteresting. But, fortunately many of these variables have had a checkered past. Fertility rates have risen and fallen, while immigration has ebbed and flowed in the face of gyrating government policies and public sensitivities. In turn, family structures have metamorphosed and women have flocked into the workforce. All these changes, and more, are the seeds of fascinating demographics and social dynamics. They tell us a lot about the future of business trends and more importantly business opportunities.

Fertility rates in Canada were at record highs at the turn of the century only to decline steadily to the late-1930s. Fertility rates then rebounded rapidly in the 1940s until the early-1960s, since when rates have declined steadily. Fertility rates today seem to be leveling off at about 1.6-1.8 children per female of childbearing age. Within this volatile pattern of fertility rates are born the baby-boom, the baby-bust and the baby-boom "echo" or "pimple." Although the baby-boom was created out of rebounding fertility rates, it was not, however, an era of large families. It was actually characterized by an increase in the population marrying, and having moderately sized, rather than large families.

The baby-boom generation was actually conceived during the halcyon years of 1947-1966, with women of childbearing age having about three children. Post-1966, the fertility rate started to decline below three children to create a small cohort of baby-busters from about 1967-1980. The decline actually continues to the present day, although there are signs that the fertility rate is stabilizing around 1.6-1.8 children per female of childbearing age. This alone is actually inadequate to sustain growth in Canada's population.

Post-1980, the very large number of baby-boomers started to have children - not many, but their sheer numbers have created a baby-boomlet or echo. This will continue until the late-1990s, when absolute births will decline again, as the small baby-bust cohort enters prime family creation stage. All this is very predictable stuff.

The Socio-Economic Life Cycle

Bulges and contractions in population make life interesting, especially demographics. To reveal its power all we need to do is superimpose the various stages of our life cycle on demographic trends. Bingo - welcome to the world of applied demographics. We have little choice but to evolve through various stages of the life cycle - birth, infancy, childhood, the wonderful teens, youth, entry into the workplace, family formation years, middle age, empty nesting, the mature years and death. Obviously, not all will have families and therefore, for these people, the empty nest is not relevant, but such trends, in themselves, have profound implications for society.

Each stage of life has specific characteristics in terms of health care demands, purchase of specific goods and services, pension implications, and education demands. Changing the absolute numbers at various stages of the life cycle can have important societal and business implications. Infants are great for diapers. Seniors revel in recreational vehicles. Teenagers love their ear-shattering stereos and automobile electronics. Youth is a stimulus for fashion wear.

C. Vlassoff of the Institute for Research on Public Policy in 1987 eloquently captured the theme as follows:

> "Age dominates, to a considerable extent, the kinds of goods and services people require and, hence, the kinds of industries and services that are developed in response to those needs. In other words, the age structure of the population influences the kinds and quantities of goods and services demanded. A large proportion of young people, for instance, will lead to the development of industries geared towards youthful needs and tastes. The rapid expansion of the music and games industries in Canada over the past few years is a function of the large market of teenagers and young adults. Similarly, as the big generation ages, its sheer size likely will continue to motivate marketing people to produce appropriate products and services tailored for its needs."

Obviously, we do use quite different goods and services at various stages of our life cycle. This has a fundamental impact on business, markets and economics. Of course, demographic influences don't operate in a vacuum and can be modified by changing values, tastes and philosophies over time.

Along with the life cycle is a particular pattern of earnings and spending, generally portraying the hump-back camel syndrome. From low expenditures by children, our earnings and spending start rising in our teens, accelerates in our youth and continues rising through young adulthood. Spending tends to peak in our late-40s and at about 50 our spending starts to slowly and progressively decline with age. But the key to understanding spending patterns and demographics is the "3Ds" Principle - Distinctive, Disposable and Discretionary.

Each life stage has a distinctive spending pattern. Infants do a lot of things - not all pleasant - but one thing they are not is big spenders. Children are small spenders and the "spokes" mentality has given them small, but significant spending power. Teenagers have been harnessing increasing spending power, partly through over-generous parents, but mostly through their high part-time participation rate in the workplace. Spending continues to accelerate among the youth to age 25. After this "family formation" (albeit an array of "family structures" today) clicks in and spending on big ticket items such as housing, furniture and durable goods rocket. This epitome of spending continues through to their late-40s, until children begin to leave home. This spending pattern in the future may be maintained into their 50s due to delayed family formation among the baby-boom generation and a trend to kids prolonging their nesting. Beyond the 50s spending starts to gradually decline. The distinctiveness of each life stage is critical for business and the marketing of different goods and services.

Other differentiation for business is based upon disposable versus discretionary income. The difference is very significant. Many people in their 30s and 40s have large disposable incomes (incomes after taxes and other payroll deductions), but often little is discretionary because of mortgage and loan obligations in response to big ticket purchases. These are the peak dissaving years. On the other hand, teenagers, youth and the mature generation (55+) often have largely discretionary income - they have free choice on how to spend their money, without the captive bondage of mortgages and loans. These latter life stage groups, in particular, offer tremendous business potential for the targeting of the right goods and services, according to desires, wants and tastes.

All of this becomes more powerful with one simple observation - the larger the age cohort, the greater is that cohort's effect on the economy at each life stage.

One word of caution is required here. For obvious reasons this book discusses demographic trends at the Canada level. Demographic profiles in individual communities can vary extensively. For example, the city of Victoria has a much older demographic profile than the Canadian average. In contrast, Calgary tends to have a younger profile than the Canadian whole. Applying demographics to individual businesses demands a knowledge of the specific market being targeted by the business - global, national, provincial or local.

The Demographic Triad

There are a myriad of demographic changes occurring in our society today, but three over-arching ones will dominate Canadian society of the future.

1.   The Boomer Years. The median age of the baby-boom generation born between 1947 - 1966 is now about 40. By sheer numerical weight, the boomers leave their imprint on every stage of life that they pass through. Needless to say the median age of the boomers will be about 57 by the year 2010.

2. The Dearth Years. In many respects the dearth generation following the boomer generation is as important as the latter. It will literally turn our population on its head. Demographers for years talked about Canada's population as a pyramid, with a relatively small number of older people at the apex, with a general enlarging of age groups towards a wide base of youngsters. We are a pyramid no more — the base is narrowing and the middle is widening. Middle age spread is taking over and our demographic pyramid is becoming a "Chinese vase." The implications are obvious; as we move into the third millennium, smaller cohorts of workers will be supporting an expanding coterie of aging people. We will need to re-define the world of work, including our definition of retirement.

3. The Silver Tide captures the significant aging of Canadian society. The median age of Canada's population has already risen from 25 in the mid-1960s to about 32 today. By 2010, it will likely be about 40. Even more significantly the number of people over 50 will increase from 26 percent of the population today to about 38 percent of the population by 2010, and maybe half the population by 2035.

Boomers, Busters and Their Echoes

Born between 1947 and 1966? You're a boomer. Born between 1967-1979? You're a buster. Post-1980 births are part of the new wave of boomlets or baby-boom echo. In the late-1990s will be born the first of the bustlets or the baby-bust echo generation.

All this is neatly predictable and it all gives a very distinctive structure to Canada's population. First of all the importance of the boomers is not that they are unique, but they are numerous. As the baby-boomers age they wreak change on Canada's society. They produce a boom in the demand for some goods and services, yet leave behind a bust in other goods and services.

The late-1970s and 1980s was the boomer era for big ticket items. These were the years of the purchase of the first home. House prices soared generally in Canada, as demand outstripped supply. The boomers needed appliances, furniture and flooring for their homes - demand for these products rocketed. The boomers didn't have many children, but when they did they lavished upon their children the best in up-market toys and clothing. They put increased pressure on services - sports, culture, dancing, singing and piano tuition. No expense was spared to relieve the guilt complex of dual income families in lavishing materialism on the one or two baby-boomers' children.

We have now entered in the 1990s a very different phenomenon, with a whole set of different consequences at work. Most boomers are now in their 30s and the front wave are reaching their upper 40s. New spending habits and trends will emerge. The primary house price boom is over, in most areas except in future retirement havens. The primary housing market is tapering off, as the small baby-bust cohort begins to enter the family creation phase of its life cycle. But the boomers will still impact the housing sector lead by soaring demand for secondary homes — cottages and condominiums in scenic and rustic areas will come to the forefront as dual income discretionary spending expands. And even later in the 1990s the boomers will start to exert pressure on house prices in Canada's retirement havens, notably Vancouver, Vancouver Island, the Okanagan Valley, the Kootenays and the Niagara peninsula - in other words Canada's "banana-belts." While the big purchase wave for primary homes from the baby-boomers is past, other forms of house expenditures will continue to rise. Emphasis will now shift to the renovation business, as the baby-boomers upgrade, add rooms, add bathrooms, atriums and sunrooms. Landscaping will receive increasing attention. Primary purchasing will decline, but liveability will soar.

Meanwhile, the pattern of spending of the front wave of baby-boomers in their mid- to late-40s will change from basic durables to more luxury and aesthetic products and increasingly a range of up-market services. New hobbies and recreational activities will emerge, broader participation in the arts and culture, and increasing tourist and vacational pursuits.

The numerical strength of baby-boomers will lead to increasing political and social change to their advantage. The political agenda is now shifting to the baby-boomers, as more and more senior politicians and bureaucrats are drawn from the baby-boomers ranks. This will increasingly mean more legislative emphasis on youth crime, personal security, retirement programs and health care. The emphasis in terms of education will shift over time, as baby-boomer's children progress along the education continuum with emphasis shifting predictably from elementary to secondary to post-secondary in line with the vested interests of the baby-boom generation. In turn, financial services will experience strong growth as the baby-boomers start to save for retirement. Boomers are all too aware that bankrupt governments will not be able to satiate their retirement needs.

The Lost Generation

The baby-bust generation is rapidly becoming the lost generation. Numerically small and politically weak they are taking the brunt of what ails Canadian society in the 1990s. They were the front wave of latch-key kids. They are the first generation trying to force their way into a dramatically restructured Canadian economy. They are the first generation to encounter the financial crunch in post-secondary education funding. They are the first generation to encounter the notion that advanced qualifications do not necessarily guarantee employment. They are the first to enter an employment arena in which most professional fields are over-supplied. As many corporate and public sector organizations downsize demoted baby-boomers will consume "starter-jobs" and large numbers of baby-busters will be precluded entry into the normal starting channels for many professionals. With their lack of numerical and political clout, this cohort of baby-busters are in danger of becoming the "lost generation." They are the first casualties of a subtle and largely unnoticed shift in income in society from the working to the retired generation. The pre-baby-boomer generation have been recipients of tremendous gains in wealth from real estate, large benevolence from, and increases in, institutional or private pensions, often supplemented by various generous severance packages and early retirement options. The baby-bust generation will be the first generation that will look enviously at their parents and will fall short of attaining their parents materialistic achievements.

The small numbers of baby-busters, now in their twenties, does not auger well for new housing or consumer durables, although this will be partly offset by a continuing increase in the number of households (due to a wide range of different living styles). More single and childless couples will spur demand for more lifestyle-oriented housing such as downtown lofts and apartments.

Silver - The Swelling Tide

Silver will become the common hue as we enter the 3rd milennium, as the front wave of baby-boomers first of all enter their fifties and then their sixties. But, first let's dismiss a common misconception. The baby-boomers are not some homogeneous mass of humanity advancing through Canadian society with identical tastes, wants and values. They have as big a range in wants and tastes as any other cohort, maybe even more so. It is their numerical mass, not their homogeneity - that distinguishes this cohort. It is their numerical supremacy that will influence trends, markets and consumption of goods and services. In fact, the baby-boom generation is a truly heterogeneous cohort. This was the generation that brought us pseudo-customization and market fragmentation and started us on the evolutionary path to the ultimate individualist consumer.

The most important factor is the lifecycle stage of the baby-boom generation. It is this that will change consumption patterns dramatically - both negatively and positively. For your specific business you had better know which!

The level of maturing of our population will accelerate rapidly in the 1990s and even faster in the first decade of the next century. The early- to mid-50s is a pivotal age. For most people this is an age at which children leave the nest, the mortgage is basically paid off (and about two thirds of Canadians own their own home) and it is an age at which discretionary income (rather than disposable income) increase. Bear in mind, even today, people over 50 comprise about 26 percent of Canada's population, but account for about 60 percent of Canada's discretionary income and 75 percent of Canada's personal wealth. These figures encapsulate the significance of a rapidly aging population on both discretionary income and wealth. By the year 2010, the number of plus-50-year olds will increase by almost half to about 38 percent of Canada's population, probably controlling three quarters of the discretionary income in Canada. This unleashes a major challenge to tap this swelling inventory of genuine discretionary income. Concomitantly, the silver mass will be fitter, healthier, more active, and more participatory than any previous generation of like age.

The past may not be a good indicator of the future, in terms of active pursuits engaged in by seniors. Previous generations did more demanding physical work, had less conventional leisure time, worked longer hours and were plagued by many ailments and diseases that today have been eradicated or are curable. Today's generation has the luxury of enhanced health care, fitness, nutrition awareness and an increasingly smokeless society. While we are far from physiologically arresting the aging process, we certainly realize that we can delay its onslaught by life-style changes. The evidence surrounds us daily, by viewing the aging profile in marathons, swimming classes, hiking clubs and many sports. It is not unusual to hear of the 80 year-old (or even 90 year-old) marathon runner, the aged granny "bungee jumper" or the geriatric grandpa doing sky-diving. Seniors "Games" or "Olympics" will become rapidly growing events in future years.

Life starts at 50 will become the familiar refrain for the baby-boomers. Increasingly as we move to beyond 2010, for many, 50 will be only just over half of their lifespan. Decades of very active life will lie ahead. The concept of retirement will become murky. Some will select early retirement and enter an extended orgy of leisure, experiences and fun. Others will remain consumed by the pleasures and rewards of work. Either way, 65 will no longer be the elixir for defining retirement. It will be recognized for what it has always been - an arbitrary age mandated by government decree with a decreasing relevance and logic.

A touch of history here reveals the "magic" of setting retirement at 65. Its roots are founded in nineteenth century Germany, when Germany's "Iron Chancellor" Otto von Bismarck first decreed 70 as the retirement age, which German officials soon reduced to 65. This was indeed an artificial number, as at the turn of the century a minute proportion of the population ever attained this age. Bismarck had played it safe (the average life expectancy age in Germany at the time was 45). He certainly never had financial problems funding his state pension plan! For the future forget 65 - it will be just that, another number, in this case an irrelevant number!

Health Care... And Business

An aging population will exacerbate the problems of financing a public health care system already stretched to breaking point. While not necessarily agreeing with the inevitable conclusions, it seems clear to me that a two tier health care system is steaming towards us...fast. Socially repugnant though this may be, it means big business. The state will undoubtedly continue to provide a basic level of health care to all, but many facets such as diagnostic medicine, non-essential prescriptions, cosmetic and "comfort" medicine will become part of the second tier - only available at a price to those who can afford it. Access to medical practitioners will be "screened" via user fees, hospital stays will be shortened, and many rural hospitals will be closed.

Obviously, health care expenditures rise most rapidly among the elderly. Between 1990 and 2010 the proportion of the Canadian population over the age of 65 swells from 11 to 16 percent (almost the same level of Sweden today, the globe's most geriatric nation). In other words, almost 50 percent more seniors than today. The real significance is that research studies have shown that per capita health costs of a 70 year-old is almost ten times that of a 10 year- old and at least three times that of the average 40 year-old. But, bear in mind that even in an aging society it is not the elderly as a whole that consumes the lion's share of health care dollars, but a minority of the aged who are terminally ill or extremely sick. As the aging of the population accelerates over the next 20 years and beyond, health care will become big business. The real demographic impact, however, will be a 2010 plus phenomenon rather than immediate. In the short term, other factors such as cost and new technologies will shape the health care system as is discussed in a later section.

The Dependent - Supporting Dichotomy

For most of us we begin life as neophyte dependents and end life as more mature dependents. And in between we play the role of supporters. In demographics the ratio between young and old dependents in relation to the economic supporters is often called the dependency ratio. It is another important number and it is changing.

Dependent, in this instance, means the government transfer of funds through taxation from economic supporters ("workers") to economic dependents ("non-workers'); that is mostly the young and the elderly. This is the accepted framework for most western democratic systems. The system becomes vulnerable, however, if the ratio of dependents to supporters becomes unduly skewed. This is the future for Canada...but not for a while.

Contrary to popular belief the dependency ratio - defined as the total population as a ratio of 20-64 year-olds - continues to decline from historic highs. This ratio peaked at 2.73 in 1960, due to the large number of dependent youngsters. This was the peak years of young baby-boomers. It has declined ever since to a level of 1.65 today. Despite an aging population the ratio will, strangely, continue to decline modestly for almost two more decades until about 2012. Then, as the baby-boomers become seniors, the ratio starts rising rapidly and will probably reach 1.80 by 2030.

A tempting conclusion for the dependent-supporting dichotomy is that we are in great shape for at least 20 years - plenty of supporters to make dependents happy. In reality, this does not tell the whole story. Beneath the veneer of a modestly declining dependency ratio, two contrasting trends are happening. The number of young dependents (under 20 years-old) per supporting population of 20-64 year olds is declining rapidly from 29 percent in 1986 to 22 percent by 2010 and 20 percent by 2030. Between 1986 and 2010 there will be 50 percent more seniors in Canada and by 2025 there will be double the numbers. Thus, the future will require large shifts in government taxation from the young (particularly schools) to the elderly in the form of health care and pensions. Despite modestly declining dependency ratios, the financial demands for supporting dependents may increase, because funding health care and pensions for the elderly may be a bigger cost, than the accrued savings from schools with shrinking numbers of school age populace.

Undoubtedly, the aging population and a rising number of older dependents will lead to many changes in Canadian society. The arbitrary retirement age established at 65 will disappear. While common perceptions are that people will retire earlier, the realties may be different. Based upon affordability some people will retire earlier, but as we evolve to higher percentages of older dependents (especially beyond 2010) many people will retire beyond 65. The working 75 year-old will not be an uncommon sight.

The Diverse Household

While the Canadian population grows slowly, the growth in households has far outpaced population growth. This trend will continue in the future, especially with the plus-45 year-olds category. Over the next twenty years, population will grow about 10 percent, whereas households will increase by over 30 percent.

The reasons are rather self-evident with significant social charge within the family unit. First and foremost, the dominant role of the nuclear family has significantly decreased. In its wake has grown an array of different family structures and, in particular, strong growth in non-family households (people living alone or in groups of unrelated persons). The future, however, is not one where the family unit is dead, but rather one with a redefinition of what constitutes a family, and a fragmentation of household types.

Many changes are occurring to account for growth in the non-nuclear family and non-family households. The allure of marriage as an institution has eroded, with a strong growth in common-law arrangements as a percent of unions, and among people in their lower 20s it is now about 40 percent and growing. The average age of marriage has increased rapidly and for males today is about 28 and females about 26. Further postponement of marriage is likely in the future as more people strive to finish extended periods of post-secondary education, focus on careers and are content with common-law relationships.

The fastest growing family structure today is undoubtedly the single parent family, 80 percent of which are headed by females. This fits closely with the trend to increasing divorce, with about 3.5 out of every 10 marriages now ending in divorce. In addition, couples tend to be marrying later, often choosing to remain childless or delaying child-rearing into their thirties.

Beyond a fragmentation of family structures, the largest growth continues to be in non-family households. Non-family households now represent almost 30 percent of all private households, as opposed to about 20 percent in the early-1970s. These include the never married singles, as well as the widowed and divorced. This segment will continue to increase reaching 35-38 percent of all private households by 2010. Even more significantly will be the surge in the older, divorced or widowed unattached individuals. Their numbers could double in the next twenty years.

The other major change in households will parallel the trends in Canadian population - aging. Starting in the 1990s, but accelerating in the early part of the next century, there will be a surge in households with age profiles over 45. Today the percentage of households headed by adults over 45 years of age is about 50 percent. By 2010, this number will swell to about 62-63 percent. In the next twenty years, goods and services centred on households should focus on a more middle-aged household. Beyond 2010, the focus should increasingly evolve towards the elderly.

The household of the future will be radically different to today. There will be more unattached individuals and they will be older. Households will be more middle-aged and there will be continuing fragmentation of household types and family structures (including increasing recognition of non-conventional families such as same-sex families). All this has important ramifications for business.

The Colouring Wave

Caucasians no longer dominate immigration in Canada. Indeed the populating of Canada by waves of European immigrants is long behind us. The new immigrant has a different set of characteristics. They are almost invariably visible minorities, with about 45 percent coming from Asia and another 30 percent from the Caribbean, Latin America, Africa, and Middle East. The U.S.A. accounts for only 3 percent and the United Kingdom about 4 percent (compared with 35 percent in the mid 1960s). Invariably, immigrants flock to urban not rural areas and indeed close to 75 percent end up in the major metropolitan areas of Toronto, Montreal, Vancouver and Calgary.

Thus, the modern immigration wave of Canada has strong influences on the multicultural and ethnic composition of Canadian society. Moreover, this impact is focused in the four major metropolitan areas - 75 percent of immigrants are being absorbed within less than 40 percent of Canada's population.

The new immigrants are in many ways much more heterogeneous than in the past, with wide diversity in culture, religion and language. This presents more challenges for business, education systems, government assistance programs and policies and ultimately their assimilation within the mainstream of Canadian society. It also presents new market niches for goods and services, everything from increasing multicultural restaurants and grocery stores to English as a second language (ESL) training.

The Business of Demographics

It should be obvious that the business implications flowing from the cohort size at various stages of the life cycle is formidable. The previous discussion pinpoints large bulges and contraction in the numbers of people at these stages, as time moves on. Teenagers are important spenders to a limited and selective numbers of businesses. Family formation is boom times for house builders and furniture sales persons. The 50-64 year-old may be the best of all - the wealthiest segment of society with the greatest discretionary income. Demographics allows us to predict the ebbs and flows of these groups as their numbers bulge and contract through the generations.

The next twenty years will have the following major characteristics:

> general aging of population;
> aging of the labour force;
> an enormous swelling in the 50-64 year old cohort;
> contracting family formation;
> contracting youth and young generation;
> increasing seniors (65+);
> domination of immigration by visible minorities;
> greater ethnic diversity of Canada's major urban centers;
> fragmentation of household types.

Business Opportunities from the Aging Baby-Boomers

Self Development

Non-vocational Education
The Arts
Reading
Educational and Cultural Travel
Seminar and Conference Retreats
Unconventional Medicine and
  Wellness Programs
Personal Care Products
Cosmetic Surgery
More Specialized Magazines
Cross-training or Combo-fitness
  Programs
"University of the Air"
Health and Dietary Foods

Play

Adventure Travel
Cross Country Skiing
Recreational Vehicles
Sports and Luxury Cars
Cycling (Tours)
Eco-Tourism
Water Sports
"Seniors Games"
Indoor Games
    - bridge/cards
    - pool/snooker
    - table tennis
Activity-based Weekends
Boating/Yachting/Kayaking/Rowing
Elderhostels

Relaxation

Bird and Animal Watching
Photography
Walking and Hiking
Swimming
Gardening
Arts and Crafts
Stress Clinics
Yoga
Massage Centres
Eating-out
De-cocooning
Meeting Haunts (coffee/ tea-
  houses, wine bars, juice bars)
Neighbourhood Pubs

Investments

Canadian Art/Antiques
Mutual Funds
Cottages and Second Homes
Time-Shares
Renovations
Sun Rooms
Home-Security Systems

Convenience

Grocery Home Delivery
Home Health Care Kits
Entertainment
"Digital" Shopping/Banking
Personalized Television Programs
Personal Services
        - housecleaning
        - landscaping/gardening
        - pet services
        - "house-sitting"
        - window cleaning
        - painting/decorating
        - interior design

4

ENVIRONMENT —
THE GREENSWELL

SUSTAINABLE DEVELOPMENT

Born Again

The environment was brought back on the mainstream agenda with a thud in 1987. The World Commission on Environment and Development, often known as the Brundtland Commission concocted two words - "Sustainable Development" - which were going to change the world. Sustainable development is defined as development that meets the needs of the present, without compromising the ability of future generations to meet their own needs. Hardly earth-shattering stuff! This wisdom ostensibly launched us into a new paradigm of global development, particularly in combination with some neat public relations scaremongering on global warming and rampantly, increasingly skin cancer from ozone depletion. Perhaps, in retrospect, never have two words in reality said so little, under the rigour of more objective scientific scrutiny.

Needless to say, a good dose of recession in North America and Europe soon put paid to environmental extremism; and jobs, the economy and excessive government spending have now resumed their priority position with the majority of the electorate. In turn, the environmental debate is beginning to assume more balanced scientific tones, rather than emotional alarmism (although to be fair there are some areas where such alarmism is truly justified). More balanced observers are now beginning to realize that the environment and whole topic of sustainable development is infinitely more complex than we realized, once the whole cycle of development is considered. However, the magic of two words - sustainable development - does not an easy sale make. Global warming has been demonstrated to be on very flimsy ground both scientifically and objectively - the reality is that we do not know what the impact of enhanced greenhouse gases will be on climate change. Gone in the face of more sound scientific analysis is the earlier nonsense of melting ice caps and soaring sea-levels. This, of course, does not necessarily mean that we do nothing. There are positive measures we can take irrespective of the real trends in global climate change. Thinning of the ozone layer appears indisputable, but while recent scientific studies have shown some links to increasing skin cancer it is not on the scale of the original alarmists' projections. The infamous Alar scare was a classical scaremongering tale of woe, soon after completely discredited by scientific results.

Let us be clear, however, the environmental debate has not retreated to the back burner, but rather it has assumed a more rational, scientific and selective focus. This, in effect, means that many aspects of the environmental debate have entered mainstream thinking in most industrialized nations and there is little question that this is overdue. At long last we may have, at least, got the message of waste not, want not. It appears that conservation of energy and materials has finally captured the public's imagination and ethics. Selectivity or selective sustainable development (SSD) is the key in the environmental debate, and science ultimately must reign supreme over politics, emotionalism and special interest groups with all sorts of baggage and axes to grind. Above all, rational economic analysis is required to accurately assess risks and benefits and develop a true list of priority issues for immediate action. It also remains unproven that regulation and public ownership has a superior track record than free-market environmentalism. The environmental scars and horrors of the communist Eastern block are now being revealed. The public ownership of forests in Canada paints a sorry picture against private property rights for forest companies in Sweden. The same criticism can be levelled at the management of fishery stocks off the east coast of Canada. Many of these examples reflect the "tragedy of the commons." Distant history has taught us many lessons from the over-development of a commonly held or publicly owned resource; it invariably gets overdeveloped more frequently than privately held resources, where self interest is a remarkable arbiter. It is becoming increasingly evident that property rights, rather than regulation, may have a much bigger potential for the correction of our environmental ills.

Sustainable Development — Selectively Yours!

The chart below is an attempt to identify contrasting themes of the current development process with presumably some key elements of sustainable development. It is important to recognize that a mainstream shift has occurred to embrace selective elements of more sustainable development, but certainly some still appear anathema to the public at large.

Selective sustainable development (SSD) will be the keyword for business in the 1990s and beyond. Seeking the areas with preferred pay-backs is essential as well as recognizing priority issues among a fickle public and wavering customers.

Are We Ready For Sustainable Development?

CURRENT DEVELOPMENT THEMES		SUSTAINABLE DEVELOPMENT THEMES
Consumption Focus	⇔	Conservation Focus
The Automobile	⇔	Mass Transit
Throw-Away Society	⇔	Recycling/Reusability
Waste Creation/Disposal	⇔	Waste Avoidance
Volume Technology	⇔	Appropriate Technology
Fossil Fuels Driven	⇔	Alternate/Renewable Energy
"Mining" Agriculture	⇔	Sustainable Agriculture
Urban Sprawl	⇔	Urban Concentration
Benign Neglect of LDCs	⇔	LDC Consciousness
The Development Chain	⇔	The Development Cycle
Materialism	⇔	Aesthetic Balance

Three themes of selective sustainable development (SSD) seem especially relevant to business over the next couple of decades in North America. There is a movement from pure consumption to a more conservation-oriented ethic, with strong potential for increasing acceptance in the near future. Technology will be the enabling force, permitting the conservation of materials with minimal price impacts. Secondly, there is a drive to recycling/reusability. This is becoming engraved in the new "green" consumer. Thirdly, industry is now awakening to the issue of waste avoidance, rather than waste creation and disposal. Rising liability and the increasing cost of disposal is beginning to favour full cycle or cradle-to-grave philosophies on costs of waste avoidance. This will result in the evolution from the development chain to the development cycle. Other shifts will be more modest, but inroads will also be made in terms of more sustainable agricultural practices and the excesses of urban sprawl will start coming under control with increasing urban concentration and emergence of "village design" concepts in new urban developments. Aesthetic balance will start making inroads on crass materialism.

In other areas expect little shift. Fossil fuels will continue to dominate the transportation fuel industry, with only some modest shift to alternates (mainly natural gas). Renewable energy in transportation will remain largely a mirage over at least the next 15 years. Public transit will make some inroads on the sacrosanct private vehicle in the highly congested urban centres, but weaning us off the car will be a long process, meeting with intransigent consumer resistance in most areas.

CONSERVATION — THE SLEEPING GIANT

In so many respects, conservation can solve many of the environmental problems that ail industrial societies, probably none more so than Canada. On the basis of available technology alone, conservation will be the "sleeper" industry of the next decade or so. In terms of new emerging technologies, conservation will become mega-business. Conservation alone is probably one of the most powerful drivers for environmental cleanup and rehabilitation. Its impact is all pervasive. The gains are enormous! It is simple, effective and impacts little on our freedoms and chosen way of living. It also is probably one of the best methods of hedging our bets and addressing concerns of global climate change, whether these concerns are valid or not. Moreover, critically, it enhances industrial competitiveness in global markets.

Using current technology alone, subcompact automobiles already can achieve over 25 kilometres per litre of gasoline. This is two and a half times the average automobile! New high efficient furnaces in homes will lead to a 50 percent improvement in fuel consumption. New gas turbine technology for generating electrical power gives about 50 percent improvement in fuel efficiency and consumption, compared with most existing boiler operations.

The future for Canadian energy producers will not be a concern about energy supplies, and shortages, but what to do with the surpluses!

Energy Profligacy To Energy Scrooge

The future wave of energy constraint will not be driven by environmental sensitivities alone, but also by cost. It will be driven by industry's relentless drive for cost competitiveness in a hostile world trading arena and it will be driven by the consumer's need to reduce expenditures in a world of declining real incomes. But, the environment will be the beneficiary.

Don't underestimate the magnitude of change or impact. We are energy hogs. We are undisputed world champion energy guzzlers. Technology and cost concerns will tear us irreversibly away from energy profligacy, rather than environmental altruism itself.

The Travel Hogs

The automobile hippo will become the 21st century automobile camel. Cars will contain more plastics and lighter metals, both steel alloys and aluminum/magnesium.

Lighter cars mean simply less energy consumption. Cars will become smarter. Computer usage in automobiles will spread and control more functions including acceleration, transmission systems, suspension systems and driveability. The result will be more fine tuning of a car's operability and lower fuel consumption. Multipoint fuel injection, electronic fuel injection for diesels, engine shutoff during idle, and deceleration fuel shutoff systems will save more fuel. Information technology through telecommunications will lead to route optimization, automated guiding systems and traffic flow optimization in peak commuter travel periods. The next decade will bring large increases in drive-train efficiency (a real laggard to date), and possible revolutions in engine design such as ultra-efficient lean burn engines and two stroke gasoline engines which meet stringent environmental performance. Even more advanced vehicles may include energy storage concepts such as flywheel technology to produce new drive-train systems. Paralleling these trends in automobiles will be similar gains in trucks, and buses. Reducing the weight of long haul trucks and buses through the use of alternate materials will give a large pay back in terms of ability to haul heavier loads.

Air transport will increasingly come under the conservation microscope. Intense competition will lead to all aspects of efficiency being implemented. Technological developments will continue to reduce air drag, reduce aircraft weight and lead to commercialization of new engine designs. All will result in fuel savings, one of the major operating expenses for aircraft. Weight savings will be made through increasing use of lighter composites materials inside the aircraft. More significant weight savings, will accrue through evolution to lighter aluminum-lithium alloys or composites for aircraft fuselages. In turn, new exterior designs and improved surface finish will reduce air drag, and hence fuel consumption. The use of increased automation and computerization of controls will lead to further energy savings. Finally, new designs of turbines such as the unducted fan and ultra-high bypass propfans will be commercialized in the late-1990s leading to as much as 50 percent decreases in fuel consumption.

Home Improvement

Businesses of the future will not be just efficient, they would be well advised to be into efficiency. Expect a surge in high efficiency appliances, high efficiency residential cladding, windows, doors, heating and air conditioning systems. Some of the numbers will be big.

The world of appliances may change rapidly as new designs with large increases in energy efficiency hit the market. The Japanese and Europeans are leading the charge and are soaring ahead of North American manufacturers in the area of efficiency, as well as aesthetics (design). The appliance industry in North America is in danger of being fossilized, without a more proactive strategy on these issues.

By the year 2000, new refrigerators and freezers will probably consume half the amount of electricity of today's models. Water heaters, electric ovens, dryers, washing machines and dishwashers will probably see equivalent efficiency gains of at least one third.

The whole construction industry will play scrooge with energy. Low emissivity windows with thin, transparent metal coatings will become the norm, resulting in substantial reductions in residential/commercial heat losses. The standard furnace will be 90-95 percent efficient, compared with most furnaces today, which are effectively in the 55-65 percent range, in part due to poor maintenance. Look upon this as a 50 percent decrease in energy consumption, as the capital stock turns over in the next decade or so.

Radical breakthroughs are imminent in both air conditioning and heat pump technology for homes and commercial buildings. Heat pumps, which extract low grade heat from ambient air, fulfill both a heating function in winter and a cooling function in summer. New electric, variable speed heat pumps, with very high efficiencies are now coming to market. For the near term very efficient natural gas heat pumps and air conditioning systems could revolutionize the space cooling business.

In turn, the microchip is becoming the energy optimizer. New microprocessors will optimize heating and cooling distribution systems in buildings. The new smart buildings will have microprocessors that automatically adjust lighting systems to the time of day and optimize heating and cooling requirements.

Lean Materials

Conservation is not limited to energy, but affects most natural resources products. Technology is continuously thrusting us forward to a world, where we need less to make more. Despite the criticism, many new technologies are enablers of sustainable development. Technology permits substantial conservation of our resources - lean is in, and not just in meat! In the forest products industry the thermomechanical pulping process recovers 90 percent of the tree as usable pulp, compared with 45 percent for the kraft process. Moving from regular carbon steel in pipelines to high strength-low alloy (HSLA) steels can result in mass savings in excess of 50 percent. In telecommunications, the development of fibre optics as a replacement for copper represents order of magnitudes of demassification. In future, the use of an all-ceramic internal combustion engine could eliminate the need of cooling systems resulting in substantial savings in both aluminum radiators and rubber hoses.

The new economy will have as a key characteristic the trend to de-materialization

- less mass for more product. De-materialization is clearly environmentally-friendly and the growth of materials use is clearly being decoupled from economic growth. This is being driven by substitution, the economic maturity of industrialized countries, new technologies and infrastructure saturation. Effectively in modern societies, value is being added by shifting to information-intensive products, or embedded knowledge, rather than product mass. Technology will continue to astound us in terms of ever smarter materials, product miniaturization and the replacement of materials by "invisibles" (for example, paper by the electronic media). "Invisibles" will begin to dominate our society whether they be electrons, photons, superconductive flows or genes. Materials will continue on a strict diet.

THE GREENSWELL IN WASTE

The Greenswell is taking hold...selectively. But, environmental sensitivities are fickle, and, in line with other developments, the environmental market is fragmented. Several recent studies demonstrate the heterogeneity of the market with three basic classes of environmental consumer according to behavior and values. The "Visionary Greens" are the epitome of environmental awareness. Generally very well educated, they now comprise probably 10-15 percent of the Canadian population. At the other end of the spectrum are the "Hard Core Browns," usually less educated and environmentally illiterate, comprising maybe 20-25 percent of the population. In the middle are the "Fickle Greens," that selectively buy into certain aspects of environmentalism, but may also oscillate depending on other priorities (generally prevailing economic considerations and conditions). This middle ground probably comprises about 60-70 percent of Canada's population. They tend to agree with promoting better environmental awareness and behavior, but it had better not be too expensive or too inconvenient. Thus, the green movement will only become a Greenswell, given the development of an infrastructure that embraces convenience and cost effectiveness. Invariably, the most promising area for future change is our changing attitudes on post-consumer waste. The "3Rs" principles of recycling, reuse and reduce seem to be capturing the imagination of the mass household in terms of garbage generation, collection and disposal. While the consumer pays token attention to reducing their usage of personal vehicles, the "3Rs" principles seem to be establishing the foundation of a new mega-business for the 1990s.

The consumer is becoming conscious of waste, because of bulging landfills in many urban centres. Even in areas with no pressing landfill shortages, many consumers are becoming sensitive about over-packaging of North American products. Packaging is about to go on a diet, and not too soon. The bagging of consumer purchases will become much more selective, with many people content to purchase a product with attached receipt and no accompanying bag. Waste reduction will emerge as a new environmental norm.

The second stage will embrace an elevation up the effort curve to reuse. Consumers will reuse bags or purchase durable bags. Disposable cups and cutlery will be replaced by durable products and rewashed after use. Even clothing will be subject to re-use, through a proliferation of consignment stores in the tougher economic environment of the future.

The inevitable third stage will be the entrenchment of recycling norms into society's psyche.

Reduction — Waste Not, Want Not!

The escalating cost of waste disposal, long term liability issues and tightening government regulations are leading many corporations to re-think the economics of waste. Waste minimization or avoidance will gain precedence over treatment and disposal methods. What has surprised many companies is that waste avoidance pays dividends...in decreasing production costs. This is a real Greenswell - a win-win situation.

The attack on waste will come in several different directions - product substitution and changes as well as process modification. In many respects we have become complex chemical junkies. We have been using advanced chemical formulations, where simple and benign substances fit the bill just as well. But, the first are money machines, better packaged, advertised better, and have successfully convinced the consumer that complexity is better. But, increasingly, environmental awareness and education are leading to strong consumer responses for simplicity and effectiveness.

The average home now has more chemicals than the average school chemistry lab, without even realizing it. Cleaning agents have evolved to more differentiated and complex formulations, with little if any actual performance improvement. As education increases there will be a return to basics.

Product Substitution/Changes

The future trend will be to product and raw materials substitution or modification to assimilate less toxic and harmful substances. Cost-benefit studies will become critical aspects of product use, with efficiency, at times, traded off against toxicity and deleterious environmental impacts. In many situations, such trade-offs will not even be necessary - we will just act smarter and have the best of both worlds. Smart materials will win over dumb materials.

Process Changes

The philosophy is changing - don't treat, don't create. The future thrust will be strongly towards process changes that don't create hazardous wastes. This will be accomplished by closed loop technologies, on-site use, modified process design and equipment modifications. In a worse case scenario, processes will become more abstemious in their use of materials and energy, resulting in lower per unit production of waste products.

Already the real costs of waste treatment and/or disposal rather than indiscriminate dumping into the environment is leading to revolutionary re-thinking of processes. The use of chlorine as a bleaching agent is being phased out of the pulping process, being replaced by chlorine dioxide or hydrogen peroxide - more benign bleaching agents. Beyond this, society is questioning the need for pristine white products and the need of bleaching at all. Do we really need sparkling white toilet paper (I defy anyone to say yes!), tissues, envelopes, many forms of paper and printed media? The pulping process in itself does not need to be a witches brew - alternative processes are available through mechanical degradation and a new ALCELL process being commercialized by Repap Corp.

Recent innovations by manufacturers of dry cell batteries have eliminated the use of mercury in their processing. This eliminates pollution within the process itself, as well as at the discard end by removing a strongly toxic metal from the environment.

The other key area in recent times was the elimination of lead from a pervasive application in gasoline. This reduced lead emissions to the environment; a substance which had been definitively linked to brain retardation in children. This was not accomplished without process modification in refineries, in order to meet the octane requirements of gasolines. Investment was required and, in general, production costs did increase but without any question about the long term environmental benefits.

The future will focus on more dramatic changes to reduce environmental pollution. Cleaning agents will come under increasing attack, especially hydrocarbon solvents. Hydrocarbon solvents contribute to both upper and ground level atmospheric pollution. Many mineral solvents will be replaced by non-hydrocarbon solvents or vegetable-based oil products.

Major benefits will accrue from changes in processes brought about by efficiency measures and total quality control programs. The production of in-house scrap waste, although invariably recycled, is a waste stream that leads to increasing consumption of all process materials. Many total quality programs aim at reduction of internal waste, reject materials and non-specification material. The adaptation of total quality principles by the Japanese manufacturers has now proliferated throughout North American manufacturing and resource sectors. The returns are not just reduced processing costs, but usually enhanced environmental benefits.

In turn, batch processing with its high recycle products will evolve rapidly to continuous manufacturing processes. Continuous casting of many metals is already a standard practice, especially in steelmaking. Progress is being made to extend this process right through to a finished product, with no internal scrap creation.

Re-Use — From Waste To Raw Materials

Often, one plant's problem is another plant's opportunity. Making better use of waste streams as raw materials streams for other industries will become a future growth industry. This is an area where much pioneer work has already been successfully commercialized in Europe and Japan. Not only does this resolve waste disposal and environmental problems, but it results in the creation of local industrial clusters. In short, it means local economic diversification and job opportunities.

Electric utility generating stations using coal as a fuel, invariably generate large quantities of fly ash. Fly ash is an excellent waste stream amenable to brick manufacturing for the construction industry. Brick will assume increasing importance in future residential and commercial construction as a durable, low maintenance and long-life building material, as well as an aesthetically appealing material. In future, the electric utility industry will come under increasing pressure to recover the sulphur content within the coal. New technologies, such as fluidized bed combustion systems accomplish this by absorption of the sulphur in limestone beds to create "waste" calcium sulfate. This is basically gypsum - a fire proof building material for wall construction.

Cement plants are the "bottom feeders" of the energy world. Cement manufacture is an energy intensive process and energy is the biggest cost to a cement producer. The cement kiln is a most forgiving beast and will consume a tremendous range of energy containing "waste" materials such as conventional fuels, coke, tires, organic solvents and organic waste streams. The extremely high temperatures of combustion (1400° C) make these kilns ideal safe environments for consuming many waste organic streams under controlled conditions. One industry's problem becomes the cement industry's benefit - at the right transaction price! In future, do cement plants form a nucleus for attracting certain types of industrial clusters, combining ease of disposal of waste streams with cheap economics for cement plants? Taken to an extreme, cement plants could be paid for waste destruction - a complete turnaround for the energy intensive cement-making process used to seeing energy as its major cost.

Compost and Mulch

While other materials, particularly paper and plastics, attract the most attention in municipal landfills, the largest component is normally simple garden waste and refuse. In most landfills, garden waste comprises over 20 percent of the total waste stream in landfills on a weight basis. This will stimulate increasing interest in either personal or communal composting and/or mulching systems. Yard waste itself usually comprises grass clippings (the predominant culprit), leaves and brush.

Yard waste will become an increasing target for reduction. Already in the U.S.A. many states have passed legislation banning yard wastes from landfills. This will increase pressure throughout North America for at source or communal solutions. Individual compost bins will proliferate, but are only a partial answer. More communal approaches will be sought through curbside collection for removal to a central community composting centre or a communal mulching system. Porta-mulchers will be developed that collect from the curbside, do in-vehicle mulching for use as soil enhancers or serving as a base for hydro-seeding.

Homogenizing Our Wares

Reusability of our products is beginning to focus our attention on the product itself. It is amazing that in many instances we have strived for heterogeneity rather than homogeneity. The first plastic drinking bottles that were marketed contained three different materials - two different plastics for the main bottle body and its base, and an aluminum cap. This was a recycling nightmare, easily resolved by manufacturing a uni-plastic bottle.

Extending this principle to more complex consumer durables will open up recycling and reusability vistas in the future. Design for disassembly will become the buzzword of the future - mix and match will become a term of derision. In particular, the use of different plastics within the same product will be discouraged as it will complicate the recycling process, add to costs, and potentially pollution, if heavy liquids (rather unpleasant chemicals) have to be used for plastics separation. Future design will focus increasingly on uni-product compositions rather than multi-material ones. This could revolutionize materials usage and end up favoring one type of plastic with the same plastic snap-ons or plastic adhesives.

While this principle will be applied where practical, there will still be a myriad of applications where mixed materials will survive. Plastics have such an impressive array of performance characteristics, it only makes good sense to use the right plastic for the right application.

Recycling

Recycling is emerging as one of the growth businesses of the future. Recycling technologies are being driven by perceived needs to reduce waste generation and disposal, reduce natural resources exploitation, as well as lowering energy use and overall production costs of consumer products.

Recycling technologies can be used for the recovery of a myriad of products in common use. These include a wide range of metals, paper, plastics, oils, lubricants, glass and chemicals. Recycling of certain products is hardly new. The scrap metal merchant, particularly for iron and steel products, has been in business for many decades. They long ago recognized that there is cash in trash. Likewise, recycling of aluminum cans has been an established commercial process for many years.

Yet, in many other areas, recycling remains in its infancy at least in Canada. By world standards little of our glass and paper has been recycled until very recently. Plastics recycling is even more rudimentary in its development. The reasons for this are many - our large material resources endowment, the technological complexities of separating materials and their recycling, poor logistics for collection and transportation and lack of producer and consumer awareness. But, the Greenswell is now taking root.

Paper recycling is already big business in many countries, generally those with little virgin fibre. About 70 percent of South Korea's paper production today is from recycled paper. There is no question that directionally we will be now heading the same way and in the process reducing our demand for virgin fibre or primary pulp (bad news for many pulp producing companies in Canada). But, it is not that simple. A whole new system must be established in collection, transportation, sorting, de-inking and processing for effective use of recycled paper. Technology itself needs to advance in de-inking and also in acceptance of mixed paper streams.

The streaming of papers into different grades will remain critical in the short term, until more forgiving recycling technologies are developed for mixed streams. Old newspapers are good mostly for recycling to new newsprint and maybe recycle paperboard. High quality papers are used for tissue production or printing/writing papers. Mixed papers can only really be used for low value recycling applications such as building products, mulch or animal bedding, but this is changing rapidly with advancing technology.

The key to paper recycling will be the development of efficient collection and logistics systems. Collection systems are now being developed for both residential and commercial markets. Beyond collection, the cost of transportation to de-inking facilities and paper mills will remain a large challenge. Fortunately, in many areas the transportation flow of recycle papers is in reverse to that of finished paper products flows. Thus, recycle papers may often take advantage of low backhaul rail or truck rates by using empty cars on return trips.

Paper recycling will become a massive new industry with a myriad of opportunities in collection, storage, transportation, processing and product development. The economics of the whole recycling chain will not always favor its use in more paper production. In many cases other markets for recycle paper will be developed. In rural areas, prohibitive transportation costs of moving paper to markets may propel development of local facilities geared to recycling of paper for animal bedding or mulch products for grass seeding. With the increasing use of vegetable oil-based inks and elimination of toxic heavy metals in inks, the used animal bedding can be used as field manure and compost. New markets for mixed and contaminated papers may also develop as a fuel in combustion systems to generate heat or electricity. This will propel research into high density forms of paper such as fuel pellets.

Plastic Surgery

While paper recycling is already an established business in many parts of the world, and increasingly in Canada, plastic recycling is universally in its infancy. The wide range and infinite variety of plastic types and plastic product forms creates a formidable recycling challenge. Unlike paper, which tends to have a reasonably homogeneous form as sheets, plastics can be virtually anything from furniture to diapers and carpeting to cups. In all, there are over 10,000 different plastics in the North American marketplace, but somewhat fortunately 92 percent of these plastics by volume are composed of the six basic resins. These are low density, polyethylene (LDPE), high density polyethylene (HDPE), polypropylene (PP), polystyrene (PS), polyvinyl chloride (PVC) and polyethylene terephthalate (PET). Today, less than two percent of all plastics are recycled - a future opportunity of enormous scope.

Yet, in many respects, plastics have been categorized as the "bad actor" in todays discussion of municipal wastes. This is largely misplaced ignorance, particularly on the purpose and functioning of a landfill site.

It also downplays the differing role of plastics in our society. The most sensitive and visible form of plastics use is in short-lifetime packaging applications. This comprises about one third of plastics use in North America, but generates probably 50 percent of visible waste. Other plastics applications have much longer lifetimes such as household wares, leisure products and appliances (up to 10 years) and many have lifetimes well in excess of 10 years, particularly in construction and related industries and consumer durables.

There is little question that plastics now form a significant part of landfill waste streams. In North America, plastics comprise about 8-9 percent of landfill materials by weight; but, for obvious reasons, a much more substantial 20 percent by volume. What is misunderstood is the role and functioning of a well planned landfill site. A well functioning landfill site is not and should not be a decaying witches brew, but should be an inert, non-degradable environment. In this respect, plastics are perfect landfill material - inert, stable and non-degradable.

The future for plastics waste disposal probably lies not in a mono-solution application, but in a discriminating, multi-faceted approach to plastics treatment. This will involve a combination of continued landfilling, recycling, degradability and incineration. Landfilling will remain in many respects the lowest value added use, but in the case of specialized plastics, low volumes, and more remote areas will remain the only practical disposal method. In many areas, particularly urban centres, and for many applications for the bulk plastic resins, there will be a strong push for higher value-added disposal methods.

Plastics Recycling

Recycling permits the best sustainable use of the earth's resources (in this case naturally occurring hydrocarbons) and potentially the highest value products. Recycling works best for a single discrete resin, but technological progress is being made with recycling of co-mingled plastics. Certainly in the immediate future mono-resin plastics recycling will dominate. This will involve, therefore, the development of a sophisticated logistical chain of labelling, collection and separation systems prior to processing. Mixed plastic containers and packaging will be discouraged. In many cases, the separation of each plastic resin by color is also important (as it is in glass recycling). The future will undoubtedly see more developments in the processing of color and co-mingled plastics. Until then, households, or subsequent processors, will be encouraged to "sort by number" (each major plastic resin has been designated a uniform symbol with a number inside). The complexity and marginal economics of this process should not be underestimated, but numerous niche recyclers will emerge to produce recycled specific resins for reuse with virgin material.

In many respects, recycling of co-mingled plastics is the ultimate ideal solution, whereby different plastics of different hues can be recycled as a whole into usable products. This will be practiced initially for conversion into lower value products, often designated as plastic lumber. While the value is low, many usable products can be produced such as fence posts, park benches, pallets, picnic furniture, flooring, decks, floating docks, sheds, as well as non-lumber applications such as insulation and filling materials.

Degradable Plastics - The Invisible Option?

Degradable plastics were initially viewed as the elixir of the plastics waste world. All we needed were some magical, chemical ingredients and key plastics become invisible or, at worst, a mass of powder. Yet again the environmental movement perpetrated a mass injustice in promoting degradable options. Better education is now leading most advocates to favor other alternatives, although niche opportunities may exist.

Of the degradable options, photodegradation, requiring the action of light to breakdown the resin, has been almost totally discredited. Except for litter, a very minor part of plastic waste, photodegradability has virtually no application. Most plastics have ended up in buried landfills, not exacting an ideal venue for disintegration by sunlight. Photodegradable plastics are as dead as a dodo, as they should be.

Biodegradable plastics have a little more staying power, but except for some very small niche applications, have little future. Plastics themselves are not susceptible to bacteriological degradation as they are very stable. In turn, landfill sites suppress light, air, water and microorganisms and contrary to popular misconception are venues of stability not biochemical denizens of activity.

The common method of rendering plastics biodegradable was the incorporation of starch or oxidizing additives into the plastic resin. The starch and oxidizing additives do, in fact, biodegrade and this causes the plastic to breakdown to small fragments. In reality, little, if any, of the plastic itself biodegrades, but it probably increases the difficulties of recycling and also may lower the quality of the plastic. In reality, biodegradable plastics are like magic - more deception than reality. At best, they will develop as niche markets, for example, self destructing sutures in surgery, but will have little real impact on plastics waste management at the global level.

Taking The Heat Out Of Plastics

Plastics are derived from natural hydrocarbons, usually oil and natural gas, but occasionally coal. The chemistry of plastics is exceedingly complex, permitting a myriad of plastics to be produced with different properties and characteristics. New discoveries of plastics with superior specific properties and performance are being made annually.

Given the complexities and marginal economics of much of the existing plastics recycling, an alternative is to "recycle" plastics solely for its substantial heat content. This could be viewed as a virtuous cycle for the use of hydrocarbon resources. The resources could be used firstly, as plastics in the primary cycle, and secondly, as combustible materials in a secondary cycle.

Plastic waste to energy plants will be developed and in smaller communities could be a source of much needed job creation and economic diversification. Incineration of plastics is practiced widely in Europe, but infrequently in North America. The reasons are largely environmental with respect to air emissions. Incineration in North America has created a bad public image - one dogged by old plants spewing forth black smoke and often deleterious heavy metals and toxins. This is obviously one industry we don't want to encourage!

The modern world of incineration, however, is a far cry from these plants of yore. Modern plants based on new technology operate at very high temperatures with appropriate scrubbers and cleaning devices that preclude the emission of harmful products. Modern systems of kilns, starved-air incineration and the use of plasma torch technology can satisfy the demands of the most exacting environmental activist. The use of pure plastics feed for energy generation makes the processing less complex than burning heterogeneous refuse and plastics have substantially higher heat values.

Plastics to waste plants can be used as a core for attracting other industry. The production of high pressure steam would likely mean the co-development of electric power facilities in the form of cogeneration plants or independent power plants selling power to the grid. The production of low pressure steam would open up a gambit of industrial or commercial business opportunities including greenhouses, garden centres, brick manufacturers and food processors.

Plastics to energy developments will develop in future, as part of an integrated approach to waste management. Solely using one method of dealing with plastics waste will not work, either economically or logistically. Plastics will continue to be, in part at least, landfilled. Contrary to popular misconception plastics in most respects are the perfect landfill material - they are stable and do not chemically or biologically degrade. But, there will be increasing pressure for economic recycling of plastics streams. This will happen initially with mixed plastic streams to generate low value added products, commonly called plastic lumber. As increasing sophistication is brought to collection, sorting and recycling technologies, individual plastic resins will be recycled to high value added production. In other specific instances, mixed plastics streams will provide ideal feedstock for energy production in incineration plants, particularly in conjunction with contiguous energy consuming businesses in an industrial cluster or park.

FARMING SUSTAINABLY

Agriculture is far from immune to the environmental debate. While revolutionary changes in farming practices are unlikely, rapid evolutionary changes of some significance are inevitable. Decades of intensive farming in Canada and particularly a mono-crop culture (wheat) in the Prairies has taken its toll in terms of productivity of agricultural land. Future farming practices will be forced to change in order to counteract the loss of organics, soil erosion, soil salinity as well as harmful effects of certain herbicides and pesticides. Pure organic farming will emerge as a viable agricultural business. Low input, sustainable agriculture (LISA) will become big business with substantial decreases, but not necessarily elimination, of pesticides and herbicides.

Soil - Showing Its Age

Like the Canadian population, the soil is beginning to age, and it is not doing it gracefully. Soil abuse, particularly in the Canadian Prairies is exacting its toll. Intensive tillage, straw burning, overworked summerfallow, a mono-crop culture (wheat) and use of marginal lands has lead to a substantial decrease in soil productivity. Since the dawning of cultivation around the turn of the century estimates have shown that the organic content of Prairie soils has halved. Less organic content means many things - increased soil erosion, lower water carrying capacity, crop yield reductions and a destruction of seedbed preparation and stability. As a result, farming practices will have to change. Fortunately, economic and market factors are compelling Prairie farmers to re-think their mono-crop strategies and return to more mixed farming and niche farming activities. In turn, there is an emerging greater sensitivity on soil erosion with curtailment of straw burning activities and overworked summerfallow. Crop rotation practices are returning with cereal crops being alternated with grasses, clovers and pulse crops. The latter are all excellent crops for boosting organic matter, fertility, moisture retention, reduction of soil salinity as well as being natural producers of nitrogeneous fertilizer.

More sustainable agricultural practices are returning to the Prairies. The trend will accelerate, not just driven by environmental consciousness, but by the need to arrest soil erosion and declining fertility as well as economic diversification to other crops and forms of mixed farming.

Summerfallow will be reduced with a trend to more cover crops such as natural grasses, fall rye or spring grains as well as continuous cropping practices. Enhancement of organics to protect against soil erosion and for water retention will lead to reduced and zero tillage practices. Different farming methods including contour farming, terracing and shelterbelts will help retard soil erosion. Minimizing the use of large machinery will also help reduce soil pulverization. Enhanced natural nitrogenous fertilization using clovers, grasses and pulse crops will also be important in restoring the health of Prairie soils. Old age deserves respect and Prairie soils will benefit from new evolving sustainable agriculture practices.

Pesticide and herbicide use will come under increasing scrutiny. Organic farming, which eliminates herbicide and pesticide use, will grow to be a very important niche business. The drive to lower use of pesticides and herbicides will also accelerate the trend to less harmful, biodegradable products. Crop rotation itself is believed to help control pests and weeds by periodic elimination of the pests' food and preventing the creation of large scale pest populations. Shallow cultivation and ridge tillage techniques may help reduce or eliminate herbicide use. In addition, it has been found that fruit and vegetable production can benefit by the planting of rye grass or other cover crops between rows for very effective weed control. Low input sustainable agriculture (LISA) will have a buoyant future.

BUSINESS OPPORTUNITIES

The World Of Green Business

Energy Conservation

- Roof and wall insulation.
- Thin metal film windows.
- Exterior wall cladding.
- High-efficiency furnaces.
- Heat pumps.
- Natural gas heat pumps/air conditioning.
- Hot water tank jackets.
- Variable-speed electric motors.
- Awnings for windows.
- High-efficiency appliances.
- Sub-compact cars.
- High-efficiency, long-life light bulbs.
- "Smart Homes."
- Electronic controls.
- Automated-guiding systems for vehicles.

Materials Reduction/Conservation

- Low volume packaging.
- Non-bagging retail.
- Total Quality Management.
- Electronic media.
- Energy efficiency/management.
- Alloys/advanced materials.
- Low-volume water shower heads.
- Dual-flush toilets.
- Bulk bins.
- Water conservation.

Industrial Applications

- ➤ Closed-loop technologies.
- ➤ Cogeneration/combined cycle power plants.
- ➤ District-heating schemes.
- ➤ Waste-heat greenhouse schemes.
- ➤ Integrated industrial complexes/clusters.
- ➤ Waste incineration schemes.
- ➤ Cement kilns as "waste eaters."
- ➤ Continuous rather than batch processing.
- ➤ High-yield technologies (thermomechanical pulping).
- ➤ Sewage treatment facilities.
- ➤ Scrubbers.
- ➤ Reprocessing of waste streams

Recycling

- ➤ Waste paper collection/transportation systems.
- ➤ De-inking facilities and sludge removal/use.
- ➤ Paper recycling plants.
- ➤ Plastics collection/sorting depots.
- ➤ Plastics recycling plants.
- ➤ Plastic lumber applications.
- ➤ Composting (yard/domestic waste).
- ➤ Mulching (yard/tree waste).
- ➤ Mobile mulchers.
- ➤ Waste oil treatment/reprocessing.
- ➤ Design for disassembly schemes.
- ➤ Copier cartridges.

Re-usability Items

- ➤ Cloth shopping bags.
- ➤ Ceramic mugs/cups.
- ➤ Telescopic mugs for ease of transport.

Pollution Control/Reduction

- Reformulated gasoline.
- Alternate clean fuels.
- Non-phosphate detergents.
- Solvent replacement.
- New refrigerants.
- New dry cleaning chemicals.
- New fire retardants.
- Natural cleaning agents.
- Non-chlorine bleached paper.
- Non-bleached paper.
- Biodegradable herbicides and pesticides.

Lifestyle Changes

- Public transit.
- Car pools.
- Bicycles.
- Community pooling of goods and services.
- Telecommuting and home-based businesses.

Agriculture

- Organic food.
- Lentils/peas/beans/clover production to enhance soil fertility.
- Restoration of natural grasslands/wetlands.
- Low Input Sustainable Agriculture (LISA).
- Zero-Tillage processes.
- Enhanced crop rotation practices.

PART III

NEW HORIZONS

5

VALUE CREATION FROM BASIC RESOURCES

The Competitive Edge

Canada is infamous for its treasure trove of natural resources. The country's humble beginnings can be traced to the fur trade and more recently the opening up of the vast Prairie lands for grain production. This was followed by extensive development of our forest, minerals, metals and energy resources. In Europe, the stereotyped images of Canada invariably involve natural resources. Europeans think of Canadians as lumberjacks, fishermen, miners, and farmers of vast Prairie landscapes. Yet in any of these areas today it is quite doubtful that we really have sustainable competitive advantage. Certainly the Prairies have significant limitations for cultivation of grains. The southern Prairies are basically too dry for economic grain cultivation (as opposed to subsidized agriculture). Climatic uncertainties in terms of hail damage, drought, early frosts and snowfalls occur all too frequently and make grain production a Canadian version of Russian roulette. Our oil resources are immense, but the bulk of it tends to be heavy oil and high cost bitumen. Our iron ore resources are pitifully low grade. And now our fishing industry is beating a hasty retreat in the face of catastrophically depleting stocks.

In reality, many of these resources did have a competitive advantage in their day, but that advantage has been receding as vast new resources are developed in poorly-explored Third World countries and new technology changes competitive relationships (for example, the Green Revolution in many Third-World countries).

The Resources Scarcity Myth

Collectively, there has been a long history perpetrating the myth of scarcity of basic resources. Thomas Malthus, the British political economist was long recognized as being at the vanguard of the doomsday movement. He argued that the limited productivity of land would in the near future constrain population growth. That was about two hundred years ago! Yet, while hundreds of millions of people are indeed starving today, the fault is hardly the lack of productivity of land or its capabilities of easily meeting global food demands. The sad truth is that these people are starving, not for the lack of global food production capability, but because of logistics, transportation, warfare, corruption and sundry political indigestion. Indeed, mountains of food are destroyed annually from overproduction and "lack of markets." To prove that Malthus, though wrong, is still alive and well, along comes the next crew of doomsday economists - the so-called Club of Rome. Obviously, indulging in more Chianti than understanding we are categorically told in 1973 that there would be a shortage of most energy and metallic commodities by the mid-1980s. Surprise, surprise that the last decade has witnessed unprecedented increases in energy and metals reserves and far more commodity gluts than surpluses. In anything like the foreseeable future, expect more of the same.

Among the Club of Rome's many flaws was a fundamental misunderstanding of renewable and non-renewable resources. There are, in fact, very few global non-renewable resources. I can think of only three major ones - crude oil, natural gas and coal. Even this needs qualification according to usage. Hydrocarbons used in combustion processes - the bulk of their use - are truly non-renewable. Once burned their value is transmitted into products with substantially lower energy value - carbon dioxide and water (at least, today this is true). Other uses of hydrocarbons, as in building blocks for an array of basic petrochemicals, are not necessarily non-renewable. Basic petrochemicals retain an inherent energy value, which can, upon incineration, result in high recovered energy values. The use of hydrocarbons as feedstock to chemicals can be looked upon as a "double-dipping" cycle - chemical usage first and then recovered energy levels as a secondary cycle.

Beyond the world of energy resources,, however, all other natural resources are renewable - metals, trees, grains and water. It never ceases to amaze me how many people conceive of metals as a non-renewable resource. On a parochial national basis this can, of course, be true, but not on a global basis. Until alchemy or other metal wizardry is perfected the global resources of metals will remain unchanged (actually through active on-going mineral deposition, resources are actually added within the earth's crust on a daily basis). In fact, a visionary would say the only real change in metals concentration is that eventually - centuries hence - the metal exporting countries will deplete their resources, while the metal importing countries will progressively inflate theirs. In 500 years time Japan may be exporting recovered copper to Canada!

Canada as a resource-rich country remains peculiarly paranoid about resource availability. Paradoxically, much more so than countries poorly-endowed with resources such as Japan. We have this ridiculous adherence to self-sufficiency - none more so than in energy. We must be one of the only countries in the world that is self-sufficient (plus!) in every energy resource - oil, gas, coal, uranium, wood and hydroelectricity. At times we feel so passionately that we place embargoes on these products - oil and gas in the 1970s and early 1980s. Effectively, even today, we resist the export of hydroelectric power, ostensibly on environmental and social grounds. Presumably, we believe the rivers will suddenly dry up. And don't dare mention water exports in Canada. Our paranoia is not limited to energy products. In the 1970s and early 1980s, we variously considered export controls on ferrous scrap metal, metallurgical coal, molybdenum and nickel. Yet , of course, poor resource endowment has severely hampered economic and industrial development in Japan!

Let us be unequivocally clear - massive resource endowment no longer gives Canada any global competitive advantages. We have to move beyond natural resources development to enhanced development of our human resources talent pool. As Peter Drucker, the noted American management consultant, observed: "Resources and materials have been decoupled from economic activity, and primary resource sectors, once the key to economic expansion, have become irrelevant to explanations of most economic events."

To prove that we are slow learners we now add a modern twist to the shortage hypothesis, the magic words "sustainable development." Ms. Brundtland should be commended on introducing us to these two words. Although the infamous Brundtland Commission of 1987 is ostensibly concerned with the environment, the sustainability of natural resources exploitation once again raises its head. The veiled concern is again our scarce resource base and a world of imminent resources shortages. But, the question is not natural resource shortages, but simply their wise use in light of continuing technological advances, lower per unit material usage and applying re-use and recycling principles.

All this would be academic trivial pursuit, if we had not, as a country, basically determined our economic development policies on increasing scarcity (and therefore higher prices) of basic raw materials. Yet, the reverse is true and the sooner we abandon our preoccupations with natural resources exploitation and fundamental processing the better. We need to buy into the new economy and very soon. A failure to move now dooms us to second rate industrial status. Among other things this means abandoning the obscene levels of agricultural support and the nonsensical subsidies for high cost energy as regional development programs. Money needs to be channelled to the more productive, value added entrepreneurial sectors of our economy. The obsession with resources mega-projects in Canada has lead to spiraling debt loads and a superb collection of white elephants - the Co-op upgrader in Regina, the Hibernia oil project (Newfoundland), northeast British Columbia coal development, the Sydney Steel fiasco (Nova Scotia), Sidbec Inc. (Quebec) and the magnesium smelter in Alberta. The list is indeed endless and entails economic losses in the billions of dollars.

What are the real lessons to be learned from resources development in the past and what can be gleaned about the future? Undoubtedly, Canada's natural resource industries with few exceptions have seen their zenith. Most are, or will be, on decline - some very rapidly. Resources, let alone being engines of growth, will be a recalcitrant brake on our economy. Resources in Canada are threatened by massive new energy and metals resources elsewhere. Many of our resources are becoming uncompetitive - certainly not depleted. In turn, we are slow at learning the lessons of commodity prices. Here again the economists retain their inimitable success rate - of being one hundred percent wrong - believing that prices would increase in real terms. Counterintuitively perhaps to economists, but not to technologists, the opposite is invariably true - commodity prices decline in real terms over time, or are at best flat. Why? It is the powerful lever of technological change - better extraction techniques, larger (or smaller!) scale, biotechnological developments, continuous processing methods, computerization, satellite mapping, 3-D seismic processing and interpretation, as well as a myriad of other innovations. With more to come! All help increase efficiency, productivity and recovery, helping to keep real commodity prices flat or usually declining. Incidentally, labor requirements per unit of output also decrease substantially. More about that later!

A philosophy of natural resources abundance, world-wide, suddenly exposes the weakness of Canada's future dependence on basic resources extraction and processing. We have no comparative advantage in the production of many resource commodities. In fact often, we have severe growth-constraining disadvantages:

> high labor costs and inflexible staffing arrangements;
> high infrastructure costs;
> high capital costs in terms of interest rates, regulatory requirements and climatization costs;
> low quality resource base (for example, iron ore, crude oil and copper);
> distance from major export markets.

In addition to rapidly changing degrees of competitiveness, the last decade or so has been marked by increasing reserves of commodities rather than decreasing reserves. None has been more spectacular than scarce oil and gas. World reserves of oil have doubled between 1970 and 1990, and world reserves of gas have tripled over the same period of time. World resources of both are truly phenomenal and technological advancement will transfer increasing quantities of ill-defined resources into the well-defined reserves category. Metals exhibit a similar trend as vast new resources are discovered in developing countries especially in South America, Africa, and southeast Asia.

The outlook for most resource industries in Canada looks at best bland, often bleak. The decliners will well and truly outnumber the growers. Asbestos is in steep decline - killed by serious health and safety concerns. Iron ore is on the retreat - a low quality reserve giving way to massive rich deposits in South America, Australia and Africa. Copper declines in the face of more competitive and higher quality reserves elsewhere, especially Latin America and the south Pacific region. The wheat industry of the prairies will contract as an increasing array of countries achieve self-sufficiency for security reasons or through use of new technology (especially genetic engineering) and production know-how. In the near future Russia and the Ukraine will no longer be net importers of wheat but may emerge as significant exporters. The fishing industry of the east coast is doomed to at least medium-term catastrophic decline, for a basic reason - fish stocks have shriveled through a combination of inept management, blatant over fishing and environmental changes in water temperatures. Our pulp industry is beating a hasty retreat in many areas through poor forestry practices and old, run-down environmentally suspect mills. Pulp mill expansion in Alberta will be easily offset by corresponding declines in coastal British Columbia, northwestern Ontario, Quebec and the Maritimes. The vintage of newsprint mills in central and eastern Canada, with their antiquated equipment and small production runs means that many will not survive the 1990s.

There are winners, however, in certain resource sectors. Natural gas, precious metals, livestock (especially beef in Alberta) and even diamonds are positive exceptions to the rule. The outlook for many niche industrial minerals also still looks relatively promising.

Substitution and materials conservation have taken their toll on both energy and mineral commodities. Oil continues to dominate in the area of transportation fuels, but has lost market share elsewhere in the economy to natural gas and electricity. Energy efficiency has quelled our appetite at home, in the office, in the oil guzzling industries and in our vehicles. Technological developments of more fuel efficient vehicles, machines, furnaces and boilers have sapped energy demand. Total gasoline consumption in Canada in 1992 was lower than in 1982 despite increasing economic growth, incomes and population. Both processing efficiency and substitution have constrained metals growth. Polymers continue to make inroads into aluminum and steel markets, fibre optics replace copper, plastic radiator grills substitute for zinc die-cast grills, and advanced composites/ceramics supplant metals in many applications. Expect more (a lot more) of the same in future - the so-called de-massification of modern societies.

Advances in technology permit the use of less materials. Steel used today is both lighter and thinner, but stronger. Electrogalvanizing techniques utilize far less zinc than previous hot dip processes. Batteries contain less lead. The trend has not peaked; on the contrary, the world of materials conservation is accelerating. Studies have clearly demonstrated that since the turn of the century, raw materials use per unit of output has actually declined at a rate of 1.25 percent annually. The technological potential of today's technologies is truly mind-boggling. Just using today's technologies we could decrease overall energy consumption in Canada's economy by 40 percent. Using yet to be developed technologies, expected over the next 15 years this figure probably doubles to 80 percent savings by the year 2010.

The impacts will be inevitable. Expect further significant closures of asbestos, iron ore and copper mines, steel plants, cement plants, oil refineries, kraft pulp mills, newsprint mills and aluminum smelters. Expect significant contractions of labor use even in the surviving remnants of the resources and basic processing industries as automation, technological developments and efficiency gains continue to whittle away at the labor pool.

Adding Value

The green shoots of the economic reformation are appearing. It has been called the information age, the new economy, the next economy or the post-industrial era. What is evident is that advanced industrial nations, particularly resource-based ones, cannot survive by being hewers of wood and drawers of water. This does not mean that all resource industries suddenly disappear into Canada's contiguous oceans. Some will indeed whither, others will survive intact, and some will be forced up-market to value creation. This means adding value in the form of design, knowledge, technology, quality, uniqueness and service, propelling them into the next century.

Measured in terms of pure physical output most resource industries in Canada will decline, with a few exceptions. Some of the more enlightened, however, will seek to upgrade their basic product into something with enhanced value. Hence the value of output from some resource sectors will increase, even in the face of declining absolute output. Quality in the form of value creation becomes the key innovative driver.

This section will peer into the future of some of Canada's basic resource industries. It will describe a world of value creation, niche markets and differentiation. While resources will no longer be the engines of growth, in many regions they will remain the foundation upon which other growth engines develop. And, of course, more and more we will turn to marketing our resources development expertise in a global economy. Canada stands out among industrialized countries in being a very minor exporter of services. This too will change, as we market our undoubted expertise in forestry, agriculture, mining and energy to the emerging Third World nations. In particular, Canadian utilities are well positioned to construct energy infrastructure in the Third World, in areas such as pipeline developments and power plants.

Mining Pitfalls

The Canadian mining industry is symptomatic of an ailing, old economy industry. It is being buffeted on all sides by irresistible forces of change, many beyond its control. The halcyon days of mining in Canada were the 1950s, to early-1970s, when few could compete with our spectrum of riches. In those times the massive iron ore deposits in Australia and Brazil still lay undiscovered, many of the massive copper deposits in Chile and Papua New Guinea were unknown, nickel in many tropical laterite deposits could not be extracted economically and who knew or cared about high quality coal reserves in Columbia?

It is hardly surprising, therefore, that "creative destruction" has taken its toll of the Canadian mining industry. As an economic force it reached its zenith in the early-1970s. Today, in terms of dollar output, it is half as important to the Canadian economy than it was then. This value could well half again over the next decade or so. The reasons for mining's declining significance are multifarious, but most illustrate the dynamics of economic restructuring.

Probably, the most important change has been a quantum leap in competition, especially from new discoveries in the less developed countries (LDCs). Many of these discoveries are massive, high quality ore deposits. Their competitiveness, in turn, is often enhanced by low interest loans, the employment of the most modern technology and, of course, very cheap labour. Many LDCs are also very dependent on only one or two major commodities for the bulk of their export earnings. This often leads to a lack of market discipline on supply curtailment and pricing. The pressures are intense to sell at any price, given that the commodity in question is the only source of export earnings. This is true for Zambia with copper, Mauritania with iron ore, Liberia with iron ore, Angola with oil, and Zaire with copper and cobalt. Exploitation strategies based on a nation's survival are very different than our conventional corporate objectives of profitability. The overall impact is generally a loss of market share in world minerals trade for Canada. Our mining industry is also confronted by marked declines in demand intensities for most commodities. Whether metals are measured on unit consumption per person or per unit of economic output, they are invariably declining rapidly in virtually all advanced industrialized nations. This is part of the trend to de-massification in our economy, through better efficiencies, new technologies and the mature state of infrastructure development. Canada's infrastructure is now mature and not surprisingly our relative consumption of many mineral commodities is declining, for example steel, iron ore, metallurgical coal, cement, copper and lead.

Substitution effects also intensify competitive pressures, by curtailing demand. Plastics and composites are attacking many markets held by steel, aluminum and other metals. Advanced ceramics are invading metals' markets. Metal alloys themselves reduce mass consumption of metals; for example, lead alloy batteries use less lead, high-strength, low alloy steels (HSLA) use less iron. Technological breakthroughs at various stages of the production-consumption chain can radically change competitive dynamics. Nickel extraction from the extensive laterite deposits in Australia, southeast Asia and central America resulted from processing breakthroughs in the 1970s. It has had a significant, dampening impact on our domestic nickel industry, which employs about one quarter of the number of people that it did two decades ago. Technological changes in steelmaking using electric-arc furnaces and thin slab casting will result in an increase in ferrous scrap consumption, at the expense of iron ore and metallurgical coal consumption. Electrogalvanizing has partly replaced hot-dip galvanizing with a predicable decrease in zinc consumption.

The tightening noose of environmental and health considerations has brought pronounced changes to the Canadian minerals industry, in a variety of ways. The first is a loss of lucrative markets for many commodities. Asbestos has become a health pariah in most applications in the industrialized world. The large asbestos industry in Canada is now only one quarter the size of two decades ago and will undoubtedly go the same way as the dodo bird. Health concerns have seen lead eliminated from paints and gasoline in Canada. Lead-free paints and gasoline will become the norm in all advanced industrialized nations and eventually in the less developed countries. Tightening environmental legislation and health concerns will continue to curtail the demand for many metals in applications as diverse as electroplating (heavy metals), dental fillings (mercury), mineral processing and industry catalysts. Environmental legislation will also curtail mineral development in Canada through protracted licensing requirements, withdrawal of lands from development and increasing problems with native land claim issues.

Finally, the environment can also create different supply dynamics. Increasing quantities of sulphur and sulphuric acid will be produced from oil refineries, metal smelters and coal - and oil fired thermal electric plants, as tightening environmental legislation mandates reducing sulphur emissions from these facilities. This, in turn, takes its toll on conventional elemental sulphur production sources such as natural gas processing, with its recent devastating impact on sulphur prices. Metals recycling efforts will be intensified to enhance recovery of secondary metal, at the expense of primary production. Already in Canada over fifty percent of our lead consumption is supplied by secondary material (largely batteries) and over one third of our copper and aluminum.

All these trends coalesce to portend a bleak outlook for the Canadian mining industry. Asbestos, iron ore, copper, lead, zinc and molybdenum production will decrease. Nickel, potash, sulphur and uranium will probably hold their own and only the more specialized niche commodities of gold and other precious metals, diamonds and selected industrial minerals will expand in the future. Increasing efficiency and automation combined with mine closures will continue to result in significant employment declines.

Metals Bashing

Nerves of Steel

The steel industry is fighting a rearguard battle against the onslaught of other materials, swelling steel imports and changing markets. Canada's mature infrastructure and the gutting of many of Canada's resource and basic processing industries hits the steel industry with a double whammy. Aluminum, plastics, composites and advanced ceramics nibble away at markets. Increased use of polymers in automobile paneling will be a major test of steel's resolve in the 1990s. Beyond the turn of the century fire-proofed plastics will start encroaching into load-bearing and construction materials markets. Meanwhile, imported steels will grab market share from domestic steel producers, especially in low-end products.

The steel industry is really a microcosm of the reformation process, as it shifts gears from basic processing of low value steel products to a focus on more sophisticated, value creating steels. Lighter, more durable steels with enhanced performance are vital, if the steel industry has any hope of withstanding the materials substitution tide. In turn, process technologies are revolutionizing the steel industry. The development of technologically advanced thin-slab casting now permits the "mini-mills" to penetrate the flat products markets, previously the almost exclusive domain of the large, integrated producers. This basically means a contracting industry - less plants, lower tonnage, less people, but higher value production. Business miniaturization will prevail as the small will generally prevail over the big. Scrap-based (or its substitute of direct-reduced iron) electric arc steelmaking will begin to dominate the industry. By the turn of the century the current steel industry of three integrateds and ten regional mini-mills will be rationalized to probably only one or two integrated mills and maybe six regional mini-mills.

In turn, steel production will go "high-tech." The new world will comprise Arctic-grade steel pipes and tubes, high-strength, low alloy steels (HSLA), ultrathin strong steels, coated galvanic steels and more stainless and specialty steel products. Customized production will "lock-in" customers, through joint product development and refinement. New rapid solidification processes are new being commercialized, with the potential for developing new, high-performing alloys in many diverse applications.

Canadian Minerals Futures - Ups and Downs

"The Pits"	"Stable Rocks"	"Gems"
Asbestos	Nickel	Gold
Iron Ore	Sulphur	Diamonds
Copper	Potash	Selective
Lead	Uranium	Industrial Minerals
Zinc	Coal	
Molybdenum		

Value Creation From Mineral Resources

Resource	Value-Creating Product	Value Creation Drivers
Gold	Maple Leaf Coin	Global Niche. Design. Differentiation (high purity)
Steel	Ultrathin High Strength Steels	Technology (knowledge) Global Niche, Differentiation
	Electrogalvanized Steels	Performance Environmental (durability)
Aluminum	Automotive Components (wheels, cylinder heads)	Lightweight Technology
	Batteries	Global Niche
Nickel	Industrial/Municipal Waste Treatment	Environmental
	Flue Gas Desulphurization Plants	Environmental
	Building Structures	Design/Aesthetics
	Coinage	Design
Zinc	Electrogalvanized Steel Products	Technology Environmental (durability)
	Coinage	Design
Clay	Brick/Roof Tile	Design/Aesthetics Durability
Silica	Fibre Optics	Performance
	Ceramics	Performance

From Agriculture to Agribusiness

Agriculture is the herniated industry that thrives on support. For a country that likes to rail upon the USA and European farm subsidy programs, we keep apace very well on most measures and in some areas we excel. Our level of support is vast compared to other agricultural producing nations like Australia, Argentina, New Zealand and South Africa. In 1992, the net producer subsidy equivalent as a percentage of production value in Canada was about 42 percent, or 6.8 billion dollars. This compared with about 70 percent for Japan, 44 percent for the European Community and 27 percent for the USA. Australia and New Zealand were prime examples of subsidy rectitude at low levels of 10 percent and 2 percent respectively. Incidentally, New Zealand only a decade earlier was close to 30 percent. Not only has New Zealand weaned its farmers out of the public trough, but it's farm industry is now innovative, profitable and not a sump for public funds.

The future looks increasingly bleak, especially for sectors protected by marketing boards and the Prairie wheat economy. Both will be buffeted on two sides; by shrinking government funding in an age of tightening fiscal constraints and increasing pressures from the international community through new General Agreement on Tariffs and Trade (GATT) principles. Agriculture in the year 2000 will be a radically different industry than today. Declining mass production in grain will give way to highly fragmented value-creating niches.

Dryland grain farming in the southern Prairies will be returned to natural grasslands, as water begins to be priced at its true market value, rather than being perceived as a "free" resource to be exploited rather then conserved. Wheat production in these areas will contract and only the innovative visionary communities looking at economic diversification and new niche opportunities will prosper. The 1990s and early 21st century will continue, or even accentuate, the trend to increasing urbanization or rurbanization (living in country-like fringes of urban centres) at the expense of rural communities. More ghost towns are inevitable on the Prairies as farmers and their rural economic dependents abandon rural life for urban centres. The marked aging of the farm population will make this trend an inevitability, as few of their children will relish the expected impoverished cash incomes of much of the larger grain farm community. The younger generation will take the large accumulation of wealth and put it to work in more lucrative value-creating sectors of the economy.

From the future ashes of mass production support farming, however, will rise a wave of new entrepreneurial niches. These will involve a new array of livestock and crops, many of which will be individually minuscule, but in aggregate will be very significant income generators and job providers. The seeds are being germinated even today. These niche agricultural markets will be complemented by buoyant agribusiness or food processing sectors. Mass food is out, niche products are in. Food processing is an example of business miniaturization par excellence.

A casual walk in the supermarket aisles today already reveals a cornucopia of new products. An array of specialty cereals, biscuits, crackers, preserves, different fruits and vegetables, noodles, pasta, ethnic food products, meat products and more. A new array of soft drinks - flavored waters, bottled waters, natural waters and exotic juices also adorn store shelves. Many are differentiated on the basis of increasing health, dietary, safety and environmental concerns. Most are flowing from entrepreneurial small enterprises.

The mono-crop culture of the Prairie economy will change dramatically. Indeed, it already is. In the 1993 crop year, very significant crop diversification occurred with a one year increase of 45 percent in canola planting. Driven largely by depressed wheat prices, this turned into a fortuitous bonanza, as the Mississippi flood waters devastated the soybean crop in parts of the USA. Canola oil is a competitor and substitute for soybean in the edible oils markets. The mono-crop focus of the Prairie economy is not only unwise from a market diversification perspective, but has also proved a disaster for the delicate Prairie soils. These soils have deteriorated rapidly in the last 50 years, in terms of organic content and fertility, much of it due to poor farming practices and the mono-crop (wheat) philosophy.

Canola provided the first major crop diversification of the Prairie economy. A truly innovative, technological breakthrough by Canadian agricultural agronomists. Yet, it has taken about two decades for us to realize we need more of the same. The next several years will provide more crop diversification. Linola, an edible flaxseed oil, is poised as the next commercial breakthrough in crop diversification. Sunola crops are being planted for their sunflower oils - an oil highly regarded for its favourable health and dietary characteristics. Changing food tastes are leading to increasing consumption of pulse crops - peas, beans and lentils. These can be grown very successfully in many parts of the Prairies. In turn, pulse crops play an invaluable role in enhancing the fertility of Prairie soils through nitrogen addition. Land dedicated to pulse crops production is literally rocketing. Other more specialized crops are beginning to be grown, for example, bird seed, mustard seed, herbs and spices as well as an important rapidly expanding new niche - organic produce.

Significant agricultural diversification will also evolve out of increasing livestock production. Beef in Alberta is big business, but it will become much bigger. This industry until recently had largely a domestic market focus, but it's future will prosper on a wave of export growth. World scale processing facilities, unparalleled sophistication in breeding stock and a high quality product will result in large-scale export increases to western USA markets and also markets in Japan, South Korea, Taiwan, Singapore and Hong Kong. Supplementing the burgeoning growth in the beef industry will be substantial livestock growth in niche production of lamb, goats, buffalo, game and other specialized meat-producing animals.

Agriculture will be a changed industry. Moreover it will change the face of rural Canada. The innovative and forward-looking rural communities will prosper, while the backward looking and undiversified will perish, especially across the Prairies. Innovative rural communities will become more than agricultural centres. They will becomes magnets for agribusiness and small food processors. They will become tourist centres with guest ranches and farm vacations. They will become tourist retreats for bird and animal watching, wildlife photography, hiking, cross country skiing, petting farms and pick your own crop trips. Many will develop into arts and crafts centres, as well as education retreats for seminars and conferences. Some will even become centres for specialized trades such as machining, machinery repair and carpentry. Rural Canada will become the dichotomy of prospering communities (the diversified, forward-looking) and the dying communities (the backward-looking die-hards).

More innovative rural communities will combine different facets of future trends. Agricultural ventures will be combined with food processing ventures, tourism (guest ranch houses), arts and crafts, and education retreats for seminars and conferences.

The New World Of Agricultural Niches

PRODUCT	DRIVERS
Beef	Lean meat, superior Canadian breeding technology
Buffalo	Health trends (low fat). Export markets
Llamas	Wool, Trekking (eco-tourism)
Goats	Milk, meat, Trekking (eco-tourism)
Ostriches	Meat, breeding stock
Geese and Ducks	Meat
Lamb	Low per capita consumption. High quality
Game Ranching (Deer, Elk)	Exoticism. Foreign markets. Health trends (low fat). Taste
Berry Production	Import replacement. Quality niche preserves
Alfalfa Pellets	Foreign markets. Technology
Flaxseed (Linola)	Biotechnological modification of oils Customized oils production
Pulse Crops (Peas, Beans, Lentils)	Health/dietary trends. Vegetarianism
Bird Seed	Growth industry of bird watching
Mustard Seed	Value-creating food product
Organic Produce	Environmental concerns/ethics Taste and flavour
Sunflowers (Sunola)	Health trends (low fat, low cholesterol oil). Bird seed. Flavoured products (differentiation)
Wild Bird Raising	Exoticism. Foreign markets. Taste
Herbs/Spices	Niche products High value-added

Value Creating Agriculture - The World Of Agribusiness

PRODUCT	DRIVERS
Fresh Pasta	Quality. Taste/flavour
	Differentiation of shapes and sauces
Fresh Noodles	Quality. Taste. Ethnicity
Nutritious Cookies	Quality. Health/dietary trends
	Low cholesterol oils
Quality Preserves	Quality. Taste
"Low salt" Smoked	Heath/dietary trends. Taste
Meat/Sausages	Differentiation
Processed Game Products	Health/dietary trends
Ethnic Vegetables	Ethnic tastes (Chinese food, etc.)
Free Range Eggs	Taste. Quality. Environmental/Ethical issues
Exotic Breads (durum, buckwheat, flaxseed etc.)	Differentiation. Taste. Health/dietary trends
Stoneground Breads	Health/dietary trends
Organic Produce	Health trends. Environmental ethics. Differentiation
Bottled Water	Taste. Differentiation. Health/environmental concerns
Boutique Breweries	Quality. Taste. Niche
Boutique Wineries	Quality. Taste. Niche
Exotic Juices	Taste. Differentiation. Health.
Greenhouse Fruit/Vegetables production	Freshness. Taste. Quality Import replacement
Biscuits (grain varieties)	Taste. Quality. Differentiation
Ethnic Foods (spaetzle, dumplings, perogies, etc.)	Ethnic tastes. Differentiation
Wild Rice	Taste. Health trends. Foreign markets
Honey	Quality. Taste. Health trends. Foreign markets
Wild Fruit/Berries	Exotic preserves spreads and syrups. Taste and flavour

Big Rock Brewery, Calgary, Alberta - Microbrewer par excellence

Big Rock is symbolic of the New Age microbusiness. It is small, focussed and emphasizes product differentiation, exceptional quality and operates in well-defined market niches (including the USA). Big Rock started operations in 1984 and today is a 16 million dollar enterprise, growing at 25-30 percent per annum. What is remarkable is that this growth is occurring in a North American beer market that has stagnant overall demand.

Its success starts with quality - very high quality. Big Rock returns to the traditional German use of the filtration process for beermaking, rather than intensive heat for purification. This enhances the flavour of the beer and has gained the beer international fame as one of the premium beers in the world. The company is cost-driven and has defined an exceptional marketing strategy of focused growth in selected markets and a wonderful, tongue-in cheek collection of brand names (Buzzard Breath, Warthog Ale and Albino Rhino) as well as the more conventional big sellers of Traditional Ale, Pale Ale and XO Lager.

The company's brewery is located at Calgary and its current markets embrace Alberta, Pacific Northwest, California and soon other Canadian provinces. It has also entered into a joint venture with Hudepohl-Schoenling Brewing Company of Cincinnati, giving it access to a new market of 30 eastern U.S. states.

Paper Cuts

The pulp and paper industry will also undergo severe rationalization and downsizing in the 1990s, precipitated by inefficient and antiquated production facilities, contracting resource availability and technological and environmental changes.

Receding forests and poor forest management and silviculture practices will compel retrenchment. In many areas of coastal British Columbia, northwestern Ontario, and parts of Quebec and the Maritimes it is really quite simple - no trees, no pulp! The economics of cutting smaller trees and trucking trees longer distances to old, environmentally dubious mills will lead to a contracting industry. A recent shift to heli-logging practices in British Columbia to reduce environmental concerns and access more distant resources is an act of desperation. Heli-logging is competitively unsustainable. In part, this contraction at the overall Canadian level will be offset by a production shift to the virgin forests of northern Alberta - the new locus for an expanding pulp and paper industry.

The Canadian forest products industry's problems start with the basic resource. The lack of an integrated and coordinated government-industry approach to forest management, reforestation and silviculture practices will curtail future forest exploitation. In many provinces, forestry development is already pushing against annual allowable cuts and the resources being tapped are either evermore distant or of declining quality. In many cases the annual allowable cuts have been set too high and will be reduced in the imminent future in many provinces. Rectification of past ills in terms of unsustainable forest practices are counted not in years, but decades. There is an inevitability in terms of not only a contracting resource base, but also a substantial decline in international competitiveness.

The provinces have ostensibly managed Canada's forests on the basis of the concept of "sustained yield." As the term implies the objective is a continuous, uninterrupted harvest to sustain a thriving competitive long-term forest products sector. In reality, we have sustained a booming short-term industry, which has harvested resources well beyond the long-term sustainable harvest level. For example, the annual timber harvest in British Columbia virtually doubled between 1975 and 1985. Other provinces in eastern Canada are also now reaping the impacts of similar forestry over-development. The future is very predictable - too few trees will mean a significantly smaller industry.

Instantaneous enlightened policies will not change this inevitability. We have destroyed the inherent balance of the natural forest. A truly sustainable forest comprises trees of a succession of age classes, permitting a continuous resource of trees for harvesting each year. In reality, the virgin forests of large trees have been gutted, leaving forest companies to forage on inferior second-growth stands of smaller size and lower quality timber. In turn, the competitiveness of the industry is impaired. Except for the Prairie provinces, annual allowable cuts in probably all other provinces will decline. Combine this with the declining quality of the resource base, ever-expanding distances for harvesting and a greater environmental consciousness and we are looking at a significant decline in the forest products industry, especially jobs.

Shifting competitiveness will continue to hinder the established industry, however, as pulp and newsprint mills in many areas become latent fossils of neglect. Productivity at many mills is sub-optimal due to small scale, antiquated production facilities, especially in the newsprint industry of central and eastern Canada. New high production mills in the southern United States with cheaper financing, lower capital costs, new technology and large scale will exact a toll on the Canadian pulp and paper industry in the 1990s. Together with already marginal production facilities will be added the burden and social responsibility of environmental clean-up in the mid-to late-1990s. The demands for more benign bleaching technologies, more efficient energy management, a reduction in effluents to streams and rivers will leave many mills with no alternative but . . . closure.

New technologies, more environmentally sensitive and with lower capital costs, such as thermomechanical pulping (TMP), will sweep aside many old kraft pulp mills. Many of the latter mills using chlorine as a bleaching agent will be under strong environmental pressures to close or invest in major process changes and upgrading. The market for strong softwood pulps is waning, as the demand for strong kraft paper bags in supermarkets and industrial applications goes into oblivion. The rapid growth cycles of hardwoods, technological improvements in pulping and papermaking and the use of more benign bleaching agents (hydrogen peroxide) for those pulps ensure their proliferation in the near future. The TMP process fits our pre-occupation with conservation by recovering about 90 percent of the wood fibre from a tree compared to only 45 percent in the chemical kraft process. There will be a significant shift in the focus of the pulp and paper industry in Canada from softwoods to more rapidly growing hardwoods (especially poplars and aspens). In turn, forestry will become increasingly dependent on plantations rather than a natural forest resources. The growth in demand for virgin fibre will be under intense pressure from increasing use of recycled paper and growth in non-printing electronic media. Environmental sensitivities are already revolutionizing paper demand. Post-consumer recycled paper is growing fast and white bleached papers are being replaced in many applications by unbleached paper products. White is out and buff is in! Companies adapting their paper-making technologies to recycled feedstocks or blends will be the winners in the future. Recycling is burgeoning from very low levels in North America towards the high levels of recycling of paper products seen in many European and southeast Asian countries. Hence, the growth in demand for virgin fibre will be severely constrained.

SHOWCASE

Quno Corporation, Thoreau, Ontario

Quno Corporation is a fully integrated newsprint producer with pulp and paper mills in Thorold, Ontario and Baie-Comeau, Quebec. The company's major shareholder is Tribune Company, a significant newspaper publisher in the USA. The emerging pressures from an environmentally sensitized public is compelling many publishers to increase the use of post-consumer newsprint in their products. Thus, Quno has been a leader in North America in the processing and incorporation of recycled and post-consumer newspaper in its production process.

The company has a wholly-owned subsidiary called Quebec and Ontario Recycling Limited which operates a large multi-material recycling plant. As the recycling technology evolves, the company has increased its recycled content and has developed the capability of utilizing mixed paper streams for final product production.

QUNO has been a pioneer in paper recycling. The company first started to blend recycled newspapers with virgin wood pulp at its Thorold mill in 1982. As part of an incremental program of increasing dedication to recycled fibre, QUNO installed a de-inking plant in 1987. With further research and development QUNO can now also use coated papers (magazines) from curbside collection programs as part of its recycled blend. As of 1993, the company's recycling capacity will be about 70 percent of its finished product, comprising about 75 percent newspaper and 25 percent magazines. QUNO is doing today what most paper manufacturers will be doing in the future - setting a new environmental standard for recycling paper, reducing landfill requirements, and also significantly reducing energy and water consumption compared with production of paper from virgin fibre.

Environmental pressures on the Canadian forest industry will increase from both Canadians themselves and purchasers of our products overseas. International pressure will intensify on corporations for both the environmental clean up of kraft mills, as well as addressing their clear-cutting forest practices. Major changes in both will be required to keep our markets or we will face a rapidly contracting industry with severe regional economic impacts.

6

DESIGNING OUR FUTURE

Designing Our Future

Design is not just style. It embodies a lot more knowledge than style itself. Design incorporates new technology, which reflects itself as innovation in production, products, storage, service and distribution.

Good design is a fusion of three key ingredients:

> ➢ humanizing, problem solving characteristics;
> ➢ innovation;
> ➢ aesthetic qualities.

Design will be the hot topic of the 1990s. Design is an essential ingredient of the new economy. It is knowledge-input intensive. Design is ultimately a statement of human values. It is the bridge between human values and bottom line economics. Together, product interactions and human values define a matrix describing all facets of customers' experience with the product. Design is the glue that is reflected in a holistic product value analysis.

All products are a combination of four desired attributes:

> ➢ they have a purpose (the rationality component);
> ➢ they have a physical component (the ergonomic function);
> ➢ they have a cognitive perspective (the learning mode);
> ➢ they have aesthetic appeal (the emotional aspect).

Total design will always include the driving concern of human compatibility.

The future is design. It will continue to expand beyond its traditional boundaries. Design is not merely a specialized craft, but a creative vehicle for resolving complex problems of human experience. It will continue to open up new opportunities for non-durable and durable products' merchandising, information and industrial design.

The future of design is propelled by three powerful drivers in North America:

> ➢ a rapidly aging population;
> ➢ an increasingly eco-sensitive population;
> ➢ a population turned on by aesthetics or style.

The first two drivers concern functionality, both the rational and ergonomic - designing better products for people and society. Beyond pure functionality, however, is style. And . . . style matters. Style will sell even more and become a prerequisite in many products of the future. The baby-boom generation is becoming more demanding and is directing the redesigning of North America goods production. Witness the new wave of European products with their emphasis on design - kitchenware, appliances, kitchen design, lamps, pottery, glassware, cutlery and innumerable other products. North American producers must become enlightened and recognize that a quality, well functioning product is not enough. Design sells and the consumer of the 1990s will pay. Design must become a total human experience.

Take the typical North American large appliance. It is functional, good quality and good value for money . . . but the style! It, like the North American automobile industry of the 1980s, is on the verge of massive competition from higher priced, but design conscious imports from Europe and Japan. Design or perish - the writing is on the wall. Aesthetics sell and will sell much more in the design conscious years ahead. Part of this dilemma for us is a mental leap in regarding a large appliance as just a basic processed product (old economy thinking) rather than a more holistically created product with design knowledge-intensity and aesthetic attributes (the new economy thinking).

Ergonomics

Increasing global competition is a reality, accentuated by the rapidly developing wave of newly-industrialized countries (NICs). As a nation we continue to strive to maintain a competitive edge through value-adding concepts, technological innovation, research and development as well as upgrading the education and skills of our workforce.

Ergonomics has been a much neglected area of design, yet it has the capability of significantly increasing worker productivity. Ergonomics is derived from two Greek words - ergon, meaning work and nomos, meaning natural laws. Ergonomics is a sub-set of design, which basically harmonizes the fit between the worker and the job function. There is no doubt that optimal ergonomic principles can greatly enhance worker comfort, productivity and reduce loss time injuries or stress.

The fundamental neglect of ergonomic principles in workplace design is now

---

beginning to manifest itself in increasing incidence of chronic injuries. Particularly vulnerable are workers involved in repetitive activities over extended periods of time. The results are now emerging in terms of prevalent repetitive strain injuries (RSI). The problem is widespread in the office, factory, construction and service sectors. At best, poorly designed workplaces or equipment lead to fatigue, but more often workers may suffer swelling, numbness, aches or pain. Some of the injuries may be permanently disabling.

SHOWCASE

Cuddy Foods Limited, London, Ontario

An extreme case of RSI was reported in the Globe and Mail on November 05, 1993 in relation to Cuddy Foods Limited, a major poultry processing company in London, Ontario. In the late-1980s, Cuddy Foods employed about 750 people. At that time it was experiencing a loss of about 44 workers a month, through disabling injuries, of which 73 percent were repetitive strain injuries.

After hiring an ergonomics specialist, Cuddy spent over one million dollars on re-designing its equipment and work stations to reduce fatigue and the development of on-the-job debilitating injuries. The program has paid enormous dividends and since 1991 its overall injured-worker count has plummeted to zero. The company estimates a six-fold pay-back on its investment in terms of increased productivity and reduced work-time losses.

RSI is not just prevalent in factories, but has become a serious problem in the office as the computer has become the centrepiece of office work. The result has been increasing incidence of fatigue, eye strain, back injuries and especially carpal tunnel syndrome (CTS). The problems can invariably be traced back to faulty design of the work stations.

The power of ergonomics in terms of enhancing worker productiivity will be reflected in a growth industry in the 1990s. Office furniture will be redesigned and both chairs and desks will be height-adjustable. Computer terminals will ideally be located about 50-70 centimetres from the operator's eyes and the keyboard will ideally be about 68 centimetres from the floor. Video-display terminals (VDTs) should also be set up to minimize glare, radiation, and screen brightness should blend with the ambient light level of the office.

The high-touch science of ergonomics has a bright future and will lead to a redesign of factories, industrial processes and offices. Ergonomics will create a new service-oriented industry, as well as catalysing a whole suite of design changes in factories, processes, furniture, electronic equipment, noise, lighting and other environmental factors detrimental to safety, health and worker productivity.

Quality

The 1980s was the era of quality recognition, with an array of new processes centred around Total Quality Management (TQM). In reality, the new world of quality, however, is leading to a re-birth of design. In short, design begets quality. In turn, there is a backlash against complexity - the 1990s will be the age of simplicity. Simplicity of design is often paralled by simplicity of manufacturing, which, in turn, means lower cost and enhanced competitiveness. The 1990s' consumer will be demanding quality in terms of reliable performance, durability, ease of repair and style - in other words a premium on design. The quality era is now a catalyst for the new design age.

Continuous improvement has become the new lexicon on change. This is an on-going search for design enhancement. It has brought us flexible manufacturing processes that permit the creation of infinite varieties, customized to individual consumer's tastes. Continuous improvement is about experimentation, tinkering and continuous innovation - a different style, a better designed process and a better product. Design is about ideas and it is the integral ingredient of the new knowledge-intensive future economy. Above all it will mean the design of more customer-friendly products - stress deflators not stress enhancers.

Age Design

A further revolution will spur the design wave in North America - the rapid aging of the population. We need only look at the elder states of Europe - notably Sweden, Norway, Germany and the United Kingdom - to observe the design trends. It is an irreversible fact of nature that as we age our bodies don't function as well. Tell me about me - I continue to fight the unfightable! We know that the aging process reduces vision, hearing and certain types of mobility such as flexibility and dexterity. Some of these factors can be slowed, but none can be stopped.

It is not difficult to visualize massive design changes in response to the greying of a population. The redesign of products to focus on ease of use, convenience, comfort, control and independence.

Design Trends For An Aging Society

The age of a society is, in part, reflected in the design of its goods and services. From the size of printed materials and signage to the brightness of light in our homes, offices and malls to the ease of opening packaging - all this had been geared in North America to a younger populace. One has only to visit one of the "old" countries in Europe, however, to perceive radical departures in design. In many respects this is a precursor of changes we will see in North America over the next decade or so. A business person can do little better than plagiarize upon European business ideas for older populations - they have been there for a while.

The speed and onset of age is quite specific for each individual, but some over-arching global characteristics are observable. There is also little doubt today that the very model of a 60 year-old person is very different from previous generations - generally fitter, more active and healthier. Yet, aging is inevitable and begins a lot earlier than most of us appreciate, the notable examples being vision and hearing. For most of us a certain loss of mobility also occurs, irrespective of our fitness level. There are few 60 year-old football players. Our reactions get progressively slower, explaining why Indianapolis racing drivers tend to be in their 20s and 30s and not their 60s.

With the aging of the baby-boomers, we are now reaching a critical mass for compelling design changes and their associated business opportunities. Both vision and hearing start to decline in most individuals at quite a young age. The lens itself undergoes several physical changes including a loss of elasticity, hardening, thickening and it also discolors (it seems to do everything, except fall out of its socket!). Visual acuity starts to diminish in our teens and the size of the pupil gradually contracts. A smaller pupil allows passage of less light. No surprise that it has been estimated that the average 60 year-old requires about three times as much light as a 20 year-old. This should be good news for electric power generators! In turn, as we age, adaptation to darkness is also retarded with the onset of physical changes to the pupil. Research has demonstrated that the light on the target luminance must be doubled for every 13 years of age. Even our color perception starts deteriorating beyond 30. The first to go is the blue-green distinction, followed in our 50s by a fading red-green distinction (watch those traffic lights!).

Eye muscles also deteriorate with age, resulting in minor lens distortion and hence hinders the focusing ability of the eye. The near point of this accommodation process starts receding at a young age. In our teens, on average, it is 8 centimetres, but by the age of 50 it is about 50 centimetres. This is the extended arm syndrome or nearsightedness and time for reading glasses (or putting your arms on the rack!). Aging eyes also become sensitive to glare and a progressive loss of contrast sensitivity.

The aging process also takes its toll on hearing. Our hearing actually starts on its downward path in our teens, and its decline is most acute in the high frequency range. By the age of 50, hearing impairment is noticeable in any adverse situation. Background noise can be irritating, high frequencies inaudible, and listening to a specific sound in a mélange of noise can become very tiring. Historical evidence suggests that the hearing of males deteriorates more rapidly than females. It is unclear whether this is a genetic trait or the environmental influence of the workplace or that males are just plain poor listeners!

Finally, various aspects of mobility and dexterity are adversely affected by age, although there is substantial variation here. To varying degrees, however, the aging process takes its toll on strength, dexterity, sensitivity, coordination, reaction time and mobility. In particular, studies have shown significant deterioration in turning and screwing strength, as well as grip. This has obvious implications for the design of a myriad of everyday consumer products.

In terms of business opportunities there are many implications. North American design is overwhelmingly for the young, but aging will compel a metamorphosis in design. As the baby-boomers have already redefined other elements of society, their impact will be shortly felt in the area of design. Moreover, scale economies will probably encourage reconsideration on design for all age groups, rather than bifurcate design into old and young. Why design door handles as knobs and levers, when levers are perfectly functional for all age groups?

BUSINESS OPPORTUNITIES

Vision Enhancement

> ➢ Brighter, but non-glare lighting at home, in the office, and public places.
> ➢ Larger signage and better strategic positioning of signs.
> ➢ Use of contrasting colors.
> ➢ Light sensitive, light adjusting eyewear for both light and darkness.
> ➢ Light dimmers - adjust light for different activities (reading, watching television).
> ➢ Use of non-reflective surfaces.
> ➢ Clearer print materials - easy to read fonts, line spacing, weight of type.
> ➢ Ensure sufficient contrast between feature and background.

Sound Alert

> ➢ Emphasize lower frequency tones for alarms, bells, telephones and voices.
> ➢ Miniaturization of hearing aids - microchip technology within the ear canal.
> ➢ Emphasize ergonomic design - roundtable or square meetings rather than long, elongate setups.
> ➢ Redesign tones of major electronic systems - radio, television, high fidelity equipment.
> ➢ Ear plugs for protection from loud noise.
> ➢ Reduction in ambient, background noise and humming.
> ➢ Better designed open-plan offices to reduce lateral noise interference.
> ➢ Noise-excluding car interiors for conversational ease.
> ➢ Devices with sound adjusting switches.

Mobility and Dexterity

> Packages/containers that have handles or can be gripped comfortably with one hand.
> Larger buttons on clothing or replacement by Velcro or snaps.
> Long handle shoe horns.
> Closet and kitchen redesign with ease of access to drawers, shelves and corners.
> Higher drawers or drawers that swing out and up.
> Lighter cooking utensils (especially frying pans, pots, saucepans).
> Button-start lawn mowers.
> Non-bending garden tools.
> Elastic shoe/boot laces.
> Door levers rather than knobs.
> Levered or spoked taps rather than round ones.
> Higher toilets.
> Safety rails in showers/bathtubs.
> Easy to remove packaging.
> Larger, easy to remove caps/tops.
> Crank-operated windows.
> Motorized extension ladders.
> Built-in seats in showers.
> Ergonomic chair design and car seats.
> Voice-activated appliances.
> Built-in jack systems for cars.
> Larger-faced dials, dashboards, clock faces.
> Non-slip flooring.
> Upright freezers for ease of access.
> Lower stairs or replace with ramps and hand rails (services the handicapped as well).
> Better sound-proofing of telephone boxes.
> Better access systems for public transit (no steps or gaps between platform and trains).
> Accessible bells and emergency alarms on buses and trains.
> Looser clothing.
> User-friendly electronics and larger controls.
> Wall appliances are better than floor mounted.

Ecological Design

Finally, the field of the environment and ecology will influence future product design. A more eco-sensitive population will demand changes in products, more in keeping with a sustainable economy. Design will be at the forefront of the eco-revolution.

Ecological factors will demand the incorporation of the following features into future production/product designs:

1. increasing durability;
2. increasing re-use/recycling;
3. ease of repair;
4. ease of re-manufacture;
5. simplicity of separating cyclable and non-cyclable components;
6. elimination of toxic/harmful components of a product;
7. development of products which are more energy/resources efficient;
8. use of more readily recyclable materials;
9. use of product design as an educational tool for environment learning;
10. adjust product and design to reduce packaging.

Revolutionary changes will be induced by environmental priorities. Techniques of production such as design for disassembly will come to the forefront. This will incorporate recyclable components, snap fits, parts consolidation and less energy-intensive manufacturing processes. It will accentuate the trend to customize configuration to avoid wasteful production of redundant components. Production will be specifically just what each consumer wants. Technology and design will be harmonized into systems that support highly flexible production and distribution to meet changing consumers' wants. Large amounts of detailed information will be transferred in real time, permitting instantaneous communication of highly specialized and individualized market place needs, satisfied by micro-sized batches of produced goods. Design will remain the key to meeting the increasingly abstract and fragmented consciousness of the new consumer.

Recognizing the significance of design in the new economy is essential. Failure to recognize that the future is design will result in further restructuring of our industrial base and loss of additional basic processed production. Emphasis on design will increase the relevance of economies of scope, flexible manufacturing, intense product differentiation and niche marketing. Design is one of the drivers of value creation through enhanced knowledge input.

Design is a knowledge input used to differentiate advanced industrialized nations from the emerging industrialized nations. Many European countries, notably Italy and Germany have been renowned for their prowess in their design of automobiles, motor-cycles, appliances and clothing. Scandinavian countries have developed an enviable design record in furniture and cutlery and the United Kingdom with its china and glassware.

Canada is now beginning to recognize the power of design as a catalyst to value creating production and export trade. Basic textile production is largely for the Third World, but design-conscious fashion-wear and specialized clothing such as ski-wear and winter-wear offers growth potential for Canadian textile manufacturers. In part, this is the creative world of style, but also the creative world of research in the development of new materials. New materials allow differentiation on the basis of lightweight, warmth, rain and wind-proofing. Canada has an opportunity of being world design leaders in ski-wear and winter-wear, based on style and performance.

The future will also see the development of the latent creative talents of our indigenous people, with many opportunities in clothing, jewelry, footwear and carvings for unique, quality artisan work. The fascination of the Europeans by the native culture could lead to a burgeoning growth in native-designed products in future years.

Architectural and interior design creates different moods and atmospheres and will become integral components of the new economy. Design will become critical in humanizing downtown environments, restoring old buildings and older neglected sections of urban centres. Pure functionality will increasingly be overridden by design. Design will drive the rejuvenation of inner cities. High density housing will shift away from thirty storey monstrosities to low-rise integrated community concepts. Characterless and faceless malls will lose market share to restored older community shopping centres, as is already in evidence for example at Harbourfront at Halifax, Yorkville at Toronto, Strathcona at Edmonton and Broadway at Saskatoon. The warmth, friendliness and informality of markets will fluorish, driven by appropriate design of buildings. The market concept is a growth wave of the future, drawing people away from suburban malls to a more casual, informal and fun-loving concepts. Design changes will encourage a warmth in architectural design. Building materials will change from the cold ambience of concrete to increasing use of brick, stucco and artificial materials simulating stone.

As Carroll Gantz, Professor of Design at Carnegie Mellon University succinctly encapsulated the drive towards design:

> "The inevitable reactivation of the inherent nature of design as rational, intuitive, infinitely generalized and eternally focused on the technology and cultural problems of our society."

The New World of Aesthetics and Style

"European" kitchen cabinetry
"European" appliances
Ceramic sinks
Brick / stone / imitation stone building materials
Downtown loft and apartments
Courtyard apartments and shopping complexes
Indoor and outdoor markets
Tile Roofs
Informal work-wear (up-market sweaters, casual shirts, pants,
     skirts, slacks and jackets)
Sports and sporty cars
"Village-type" suburbs
"Theme" towns
Old-style signage - street signs and stores
Cobble-stone and brick pavements
Thin-line computers and televisions
Modular, integrated office designs
"The highlight" front door
Office furniture for the home

7

HEALTH - CHANGING FOR THE BETTER?

Natural Selection

Health care is big business today. It will be a lot bigger in the future with more choice and more privately-funded options. In many respects Canada's health care system is the envy of most countries, certainly our friends south of the border. The system, however, comes at a price. We have the second costliest health care system in the world after the USA, now gobbling up about 10 percent of our total economic output. No wonder health care is big business and will get bigger.

Affordability is increasingly becoming the major issue in all areas of Canada. Affordability will be aggravated by the needs of all governments to reduce public spending and debt loads, the pressures of an aging population, the cost of new drugs and the pervasive application of new, high cost technologies. All these pressures inevitability guarantee one thing - the health care industry of the future will look radically different to the past. A revolution is in the making. The emphasis will be delivering a more effective health care service for less dollars. This will mean a radical redesign of hospitals and long term care delivery, the development of a "two-tier" health care system, closure or contraction of services at many rural hospitals, increasing significance of preventative healthcare, a boom in diagnostic technologies, and expansion of the role of para-professionals. Pockets of private health care will expand rapidly in areas not covered by basic publicly-funded health care. Health care will be revolutionized by "healthpreneurship."

Hospitals will become the prime target for initial economies. In Canada, hospitals now account for 40 percent of all health care spending. Major efficiency gains, will be made in administration, patient processing and patient monitoring through advances in information technology. Yet, as in other areas in the late 1980s and early 1990s, information technology does not yield dividends easily. Expectations often well and truly exceed delivery, especially in terms of costs savings. As equipment costs come down, more sophisticated and user-friendly software is developed, and local area networks are installed, however, information technology will revolutionize hospital administration. All patient records will be computerized and point-of-care terminals will be installed for direct updating of patients' records. Clinical databases will be installed, electronic medical imaging archives will be available and expert systems will take over routinized tasks.

The New World Of De-Hospitalization

The high cost of hospitalization will put increasing pressure on reducing the length of stay. The move to outpatient treatment and reduced stay procedures is being driven by cost, but largely facilitated by technology. Improvements will continue to be made in anesthetics and analgesics, which will permit more rapid discharge of patients in face of fewer side effects and more rapid anesthesial recovery. But, the biggest gains will flow from revolutionary developments taking place in endosurgery or less invasive surgical techniques.

Video Tape Ops

Endosurgery or laparoscopic techniques will revolutionize surgery in the 1990s and have significant impact on reducing hospital stays. Endosurgery essentially takes the trauma out of the operation - the standard slash is replaced by four small slits, which serve as entry points for surgical tubes through which specialized instruments and a minute video camera (laparoscope) are inserted. Surgeons rely on the wonderful resolution and magnification of fibre optics, the camera, and video monitor to quickly perform the operation with minimal tissue disturbance. Newer inventions such as the wand by ISG Technologies permit superb vision for hidden organs or hard to see spots, which in turn reduces the length of the operation dramatically and causes large decreases in tissue disturbance and/or destruction.

Endosurgery will change the very concept of hospitals in the 1990s. From multi-day or even multi-week hospital stays, even for routine "pop" ops, endosurgery will often permit patient discharge in one day and will almost always limit stays to two or three days. Recovery periods will normally be counted in days rather than weeks. By the late 1990s probably most high volume common surgeries will be carried out by endosurgery including appendectomies, hysterectomies, tubal litigations, gall bladder and kidney removal, hernia repairs and selected lung, stomach and bowel repairs and resections.

Endosurgery will accelerate the trend to outpatient or ambulatory surgery to reduce the costs of hospital care, although this will have to be balanced by considerations such as the length of operation time (in its initial developmental stage, closed surgery can take longer than open surgery), the complication rates of closed procedures and, of course, the safety and well-being of patients in a quick release, non-hospital, care environment.

Endosurgery will undoubtedly lead us to look at facilities themselves in terms of planning and design. Hospitals have been established based on open surgery with extended onsite recovery periods. Most future endosurgery techniques will be solely overnight stays or even same day discharge. This will either mean a radical redesign of existing hospitals or the creation of free-standing endosurgery clinics. With the inevitable trend to two-tier medicine the establishment of privately-run endosurgery clinics is quite possible. This will offer to those who can afford it, instant care, no waiting-list treatment through privately funded add-on insurance schemes.

SHOWCASE
ISG Technologies Inc., Mississauga, Ontario

ISG Technologies Inc. is a pioneering Canadian company in the fast growing, high technology area of health-care products and instrumentation. In 1992, the company won the Canada Awards for Business Excellence in the category of innovation for its Allegro work station. The Allegro medical-imaging work-station was developed in the late-1980s. It is the first with sufficient speed and image quality to be useful in diagnosis, surgical planning, surgery itself and as a monitoring device. ISG is global in scope with 95 per cent of its Allegro work stations destined for export markets in the USA, western Europe, Australia and China.

Recent developments include the revolutionary "viewing wand," a 3-D imaging device for computer-assisted surgical navigation. The wand in concert with a video screen permits the surgeon an excellent view of hidden or obscured tissue or organs. It allows more accurate surgery, as well as accelerating its speed. Again the "viewing wand" is being marketed internationally through strategic alliances with major multinational corporations.

ISG is an excellent example of an entrepreneurial, high-tech Canadian company developing pioneering products in the rapidly growing medical field. It has identified high value-added niches, which it markets in the international arena.

Eventually, even the less invasive endosurgery will evolve into truly non-invasive "trackless surgery." Image-guided therapy will permit pinpoint accuracy for non-invasive ultrasound waves to act as the corrective beam. Using information technology and increased automation, one could eventually foresee doctors performing routine ultrasound operations from distant locales.

Endosurgery will not be the sole catalyst for out-patient or ambulatory care. Many other treatments formerly involving extended hospital stays are now performed elsewhere, in free-standing clinics. These include many opthalmic procedures like cataract removal, keratology, as well as plastic surgery and abortions. New hybrid facilities will develop that combine out-patient roles with hospital technology resources, access to doctors via information technology links and a community-based delivery system. Total Quality Management (TQM) procedures will be introduced in hospitals and will completely re-vamp the efficiency of hospital care. Hospitals will be returned to the medical staff and torn away from the over-administered and bureaucratic systems established by a plethora of health administrators. The result will be lower cost, better "customer" service and more efficient and effective hospital system.

Community-Based Delivery

Endosurgery techniques will help reduce the length of stay in hospitals. Information technology and improved management will lead to increased efficiency in hospitals. Beyond these improvements, however, there remains the issue of longer term progressive or terminal illnesses requiring extended periods in hospitals. Here a complete re-think of our current paradigm of hospitals is required.

In a Harvard Business Review article of May-June 1989, Jeff Goldsmith succinctly encapsulated our static and redundant paradigm by stating:

> "Hospitals are creatures of the Industrial Revolution. They were intended to be warehouses for unfortunates dying of tuberculosis, smallpox, pneumonia and other infectious diseases. Owing to the advent of public health measures and the invention of antibiotics, by the late 1940s, most infectious diseases had come under control. Over the next 30 years, hospitals adapted to a different mission, treating the symptoms of heart disease, cancer and other chronic illnesses. Today, however, advances in the diagnosis and treatment of chronic diseases are undercutting that mission."

Yet, the hospital as a warehouse model still remains, even as we have evolved from an era of acute disease treatment to chronic disease treatment and are now entering a new era of post-chronic disease treatment. The emphasis is shifting dramatically to prevention and control through lifestyle adaptation, early diagnostics, new technologies and super-drugs. While curability is the ultimate goal, chronic diseases are, by definition, incurable. But, management of chronic diseases and improved well-being and functionability of patients is a legitimate and achievable goal. In this respect, there will be a major paradigm shift from hospitalization to a community-based delivery system. The drivers are two-fold - cost savings and improved quality of life for the chronically ill. A double whammy winner!

Community-based systems will prosper in a world of more holistic medical practices. Technology, itself, will facilitate this shift, as well as a better understanding of chronic illnesses, better drugs and a fusion of different medical philosophies including less conventional medicine such as acupuncture, naturopathy, meditation, herbal medicines and chiropractors.

Delivery of care to the home will become recognized as a preferred form of "high touch" health care, with substantial cost savings. Daily or even multi-day visits for treatment or monitoring will be preferable to long term hospitalization. The evolution of "smart" homes with more sophisticated electronic gadgetry will permit real time patient monitoring, self monitoring and rapid emergency response treatment. New electronic wizardry will permit increasing self-care and locomotion for the infirm and disabled. Information technology will permit less direct contact with a doctor with increasing use of "home calls" by electronic mail, fax and teleconferencing. In this respect, medical care will evolve from highly centralized institutional care to a highly, disseminated and decentralized model based within the community itself. The result will be cost savings, yes, but a radically different role for hospitals and probably a fundamental overhaul of health care administration and organization. Fewer hospitals will be an inevitable outcome. Centralized hospital boards will relinquish power to voluntary, self organized community-based systems.

Along with a community-based health-care system will evolve much greater use of para-professionals such as midwives and nursing practicioners. This will be part of the efficiency drive in seeking the most appropriate professional for the specific medical task.

Wonder Tech And Super Drugs

The world of high-tech will emerge as both the salvation and bane of the health care system of the future. While many technologies such as endosurgery, robotics and information technology have potential cost savings implication, the world of diagnostics medicine, though unquestionably beneficial, may have the reverse potential of increasing medical costs. Both transplant and artificial organ transplants could also have grave implications for escalating health care costs. As discussed in earlier sections, substantial cost savings will likely accrue from the application of information technology in hospitals and clinics. The widespread application of endosurgery could substantially reduce the costs of hospitalization, the biggest consumer of health care dollars.

Diagnostic imaging will likely be one of the most revolutionary technologies of the next decade or so. Developments already permit the early detection of many diseases, encouraging either curability or, at least, better control. Future diagnostic imaging will likely multiply the number of applications and extend the range to detection of a myriad of other diseases. The implications for early detection of cancers is profound, but not without significant implications for costs. Some of these costs, however, could be offset by precluding the need for invasive surgery or prolonged costs of treatment and care for chronically or terminally ill patients. It remains unclear where the cost balance will end up between rapid increases in diagnostic applications and the potential avoidance of costly advanced radical procedures.

Computer-assisted tomography (CAT) and magnetic resonance imaging (MRI) have already made their mark. Now emerging is positron emission tomography (PET) capable of delivering far sharper images, as well as focusing on function rather than merely form. By tracking the movement of radioactive tracers through the body, PET can actually capture images of metabolism and cellular activity. The implications for early detection of cancers and heart disease are enormous. But, none of these diagnostic tools are cheap. Mammographs cost about $750.00 while PET scans are close to $2,000.00. Widespread implementation on a regular basis will mean escalating medical costs. Newer nuclear medical techniques will continue to emerge in the 1990s with even greater potential for early detection of many chronic diseases. The increasing pressure for frequent mass diagnostics as part of the regular health care system will be intense. Costs, however, may well drive us towards the "two-tier" system with routinized, frequent diagnostics, as opposed to spot or confirmatory diagnostics, only available to those with the ability to pay.

Robotic applications will begin to penetrate the medical profession in a variety of clinical, laboratory and administrative applications. Robotic arms are already used in certain types of surgery, particularly for delicate surgeries such as brain surgery, where unparalleled steadiness and pinpoint accuracy is a must. Robotics will play an increasing role in endosurgery permitting better synchronicity of the laparoscope and the surgeon's need for dexterous movements to perform effectively the necessary incisions or stapling. While these applications are the glamour ones, and hardly the norm, the most widespread application of robots will probably emerge in laboratory and administrative applications. Many laboratory tests are routinized, repetitive applications - the ideal environment for robots. Robots have the potential for not just cost reduction in laboratory testing, but enhanced speed and elimination of inevitable human error. Robots eventually will, in combination with telecommunications, lead to the ultimate in remote control and operations by surgeons from distant locations.

Andronic Devices Ltd., at Vancouver has perfected one aspect of blood testing, called aliquotting. Aliquotting is simply the manual splitting of blood serum into two or more samples for various testing. The manual process is expensive, prone to human error and potentially exposes technicians to dangerous diseases. Andronic's robotic aliquotting system is rapid, less expensive, minimizes worker error and also bar codes all samples to preclude mix-ups.

Probably one of the areas of greatest growth in the 1990s will be the development of self-diagnostic and self-monitoring, home-based technologies. This is the world of Do-It-Yourself Medicare. This will include gadgets for measuring one's pulse, blood pressure and blood sugars. Diabetics will be able to more closely monitor and control their blood sugar levels, through optimized insulin administration schedules. Self-monitoring devices will be developed for cholesterol, red blood cell counts, anemia and asthma. Information technology will permit direct communication with medical clinics for advice and ordering of drugs, resulting in a reduction of visits to doctors and lowering of costs.

Finally the human genome project is a world-wide research venture aimed at mapping the entire human genetic make-up - about 100,000 genes. By about 2005, this de-coded map will permit the accurate depiction of genes that cause most inheritable diseases. Detection will hopefully be followed by the eventual development of corrective procedures and the potential to eradicate many of the present untreatable genetic diseases.

SHOWCASE

MDS Health Care Group Limited
Thornhill, Ontario

MDS is a diversified, technology-based health care company that provides services, products and information to assist in the diagnosis and treatment of illness and prevention of disease.

MDS Laboratories provides testing services to assist physicians in diagnosis of disease, prescribing appropriate therapies, and monitoring treatment.

The Nordion division produces, markets and supports radioisotopes which enable physicians to study the function of almost any organ in the body for treatment of such diseases as cancer. The isotopes are used for clinical diagnosis, sterilization of medical products to eliminate bacterial infections and contamination, nuclear medicine and laboratory irradiators.

The Sciex division recently achieved the National Business Centre Award for innovation for the development of a technique for the coupling of liquid chromotography with mass spectrometry. This has widespread application for analysis in the fields of pharmocology, biotechnology and toxiocology.

Drugs For All

Pharmaceuticals will continue to metamorphose the medical industry in the next decade and will experience dramatic metamorphosis itself. Cost pressures on pharmaceutical companies will become severe, squeezing profit margins and intensifying the growth in generics. Delivery systems will come under pressure with pharmacists relinquishing market share to a flurry of mail order competitors. Thus, the retail pharmaceutical market will become increasingly fragmented. The low cost, no frills market will migrate to the mail order warehouses. Mail order will become the most efficient, cost effective means of drug delivery. Retail pharmacists, meanwhile, will counter the trend with more competitive pricing and increased customer focus. Pharmacists will offer more extended hours, alternate home delivery systems and more advice and consultation as "para-professional" medical practitioners.

While cost containment will place a squeeze on profits of pharmaceutical companies, evolving technology will bring a new era of growth to the drug industry. A new drug technology explosion based on successful commercialization of biotechnology and molecular biology research will bring a new wave of products to the market. This is the arena of high cost, blockbuster drugs emerging from genetic mapping and gene identification. In particular, substantial progress will be made in developing new drug delivery systems within the body. This will include oral delivery of proteins, transdermal delivery via polymer patches, specific targeted site delivery, direct genetic intervention as well as delivery of real tissue to the body (for example, fetal islet cells that secrete insulin).

8

TRAVEL - THE ITINERANT CONSUMER

Travel - The Itinerant Consumer

Tourism has been about mass. It has been focused in time (weekends and major vacations) and focused in destinations (the tourist meccas). Rather than getting away from it all, it has been rather like getting into it all. On a summer weekend, it is often quieter in metro-Toronto than in Muskoka cottage country and at least one doesn't have the "relaxation" of traffic line-ups to get there and back.

Mass destination tourism is not the growth sector of future tourism. In its wake is fragmentation into a myriad of discrete, focused components. Increasingly, native Canadians will shun the garish overrun meccas with their seedy opulence and tacky gift shops and turn to alternate tourism relating to both the real Canadian landscape and the real people. Tourism will also become more purposeful and directed, incorporating other forms of leisure pursuits, such as adventure, fitness and learning.

In line with other economic trends, tourism is changing. It too is losing its mass delivery image and is fragmenting to focused segments. The future growth of tourism and recreation seems to be in the area of the 5Es - Experiential, Escapism, Ecological, Educational and Extravaganza. Niche marketing will be the key to successful business ventures in tourism and growth will be areas emphasizing one, or a combination, of the 5Es.

Tourism has been the epitome of crassness and the oversell. The "tourist Meccas" of the world are crowded and their original attractiveness and beauty have been destroyed by blatant commercialism, overbuilding and inadequate infrastructure. Niagara Falls, today, is the perfect example of our own mecca trampled by mass tourism. Masses will continue to forage at the trough of packaged tours, quick pit stops and collection pads of destinations. Yet, there is a powerful movement, especially among the more affluent, for highly differentiated, small niche tourist amenities or alternative tourism - the trend of the 1990s. These represent the growth area of tourism particularly in a country like Canada.

The fundamental appeal of Canada is its striking natural beauty, the sheer size of its landscapes, the wilderness and its multicultural and native heritage. It is the peculiar co-existence of the rugged pioneer spirit with modern clean cities and efficient infrastructure that makes Canada a unique tourism experience. It is an as-yet untapped jewel in the global travel industry. Tourism in Canada is made for growth in the "5Es."

Eco-Tourism

Eco-tourism offers unlimited potential in Canada - a country endowed with some of the best scope of nature-based and wilderness tourism, anywhere in the world. The diversity and scale is unbeatable - seascapes, mountains, glaciers, the Prairies, the Arctic, and the lakelands. The combination of an unbeatable resource, increasing environmental sensitivity of tourists and the desire for crowd-avoidance, augers well for eco-tourism. The last person a tourist now wants to see on a trip is . . . another tourist. We universally curse the tourist, even as we are one ourselves!

The Tourist Industry Association of Canada has developed a code of ethics and practices for eco-tourism, aimed at delivery of the highest quality tourist experience for its customers. The industry desires to see the following code of ethics adopted by tourists.

1. Enjoy our diverse natural and cultural heritage and help us to protect and preserve it.
2. Assist us in our conservation efforts through the efficient use of resources including energy and water.
3. Experience the friendliness of our people and the welcoming spirit of our communities. Help us to preserve these attributes by respecting our traditions, customs and local regulations.
4. Avoid activities which threaten wildlife or plant populations, or which may be potentially damaging to our natural environment.
5. Select tourism products and services which demonstrate social, cultural and environmental sensitivity.

In many respects eco-tourism interacts and complements other growth traits such as experiential tourism. This is where the old mass tourism of "gawking" from a bus is so inadequate and where the "new tourist" wants to experience the country, its landscapes and its cultural heritage. This will mean strong growth in soft adventure tourism - such activities as canoeing, hiking, mountaineering, whitewater rafting, cross country skiing, snow shoeing, telemarking, horse/llama/goat trekking and dog sledding. The challenge will be delivering tourists to ever more remote and wilderness areas, without despoiling or desecrating the very pristine characteristics that are being sought.

Eco-tourism can also complement the desire for learning in combination with bird watching, wildlife photography, painting, cultural study and discovery. The eco-tourist can gain a better appreciation of Canada's landscapes and peoples (especially its indigenous peoples).

Eco-tourists are a different breed. They want specificity of subject and they want to pursue the subject in depth. Often eco-tours also have a high educational content and a strong sense of empowerment. The successful eco-tours are a symbiotic relationship between tour host and tour participant - a mutual feeding frenzy of the physical and the mental. It embraces not just nature itself, but related ethnic and cultural experiences. It encompasses the natural, cultural, intellectual and spiritual to produce a holistic experience.

In turn, eco-tourism like many future activities emphasizes economies of scope rather than economies of scale. Groups are invariably small, typically 6-20 participants, but their breadth of interests is large. By choice they want to combine the experience of nature with unique accommodations (ethnic housing), ethnic foods, understanding local cultural traits and idiosyncrasies. The typical target group tends to be the quite affluent, mature and well educated. Expect growth in this form of alternate tourism to rocket as the baby-boomers pass the big 50 in age.

Tourism's tentacles will reach deeper into Canada's hinterland, drawn by the dream of the wilderness, solitude and escapism from the mad bustle of everyday life. With this will come increasing development of remote lodges, elderhostels and remote wilderness bistros.

Tourist Learnings

Aging populations in North America as well as major target markets for Canadian tourism such as western Europe and Japan mean changing trends for tourism. Educational tours and visits will blossom, as people seek pleasure in an environment of self development and fulfillment. Educational theme tours from some Canadian universities to both domestic and foreign destinations are often oversubscribed. The interesting part is that the age profile of such tours is often the plus 50 category, based primarily on costs, but also the off-peak timing of many of the tours. The theme of such tours can be mind-boggling from geology, biology, archaeology, native culture, linguistics, music, art, engineering, environment, geography and history. One could introduce industrial ecological themes with visits to mines, pulp mills, gas plants and steel mills. One could adopt an agricultural theme with visits to cattle ranches, berry farms, vineyards and fish farms. The scope is truly limitless, as is the potential for new business.

An interesting implication of educational tourism is its widespread benefits - not just assisting large urban centers, but perhaps preferentially benefiting more remote communities and rural communities. The boom in adult education and lifetime learning has yet to be captured by rural communities. Rural retreats even on an international scale could be the next major growth phase in conferences and seminars. Tied in with a desire for quiet, solitude, environmental sensitivity and inspiration, one could see development of centres of international reputation in the Rockies, along lakes in central Canada or in marine locations of our Atlantic or British Columbia coasts.

SHOWCASE

Wanuskewin Heritage Park
Near Saskatoon, Saskatchewan

This world class site, five kilometres north of Saskatoon, is an example of new age tourism. Wanuskewin, Cree for "seeking peace of mind," is part educational, part experiential and part escapism (the spiritual). The Wanuskewin Heritage Park starts with the interpretative centre - a wonderfully creative design blending into the Prairie landscape in a non-intrusive manner. What makes Wanuskewin a unique educational experience is the obvious direct involvement of the native peoples from its inception to its current operation. This has ensured authenticity and a truly enriching experience.

It is a place to really assimilate the living culture and spirit of the First Nations' Peoples. Wanuskewin is a living archaeological preserve and on the many trails, which wind through an idyllic valley, is evidence of many prehistoric sites (over twenty in all). The valley is home to an abundance of fauna and flora. The whole park is designed as a learning experience with demonstrations of native cuisine, tipi building, native stories, songs and dances.

Wanuskewin is destined to become one of the true jewels of Canadian heritage. Not just an economic magnet for at least 150,00 visitors annually but a true educational experience on native life and culture.

Learning interpretive centers based on well defined themes can be used as magnets to an area and as the foundation for attracting tourists. In Alberta, the Tyrell Museum at Drumheller with its popular theme of dinosaurs has not only brought tourists to

Alberta but encourages them to tour not only Alberta but contiguous provinces as well. The museum's success has gained world-wide recognition and has been declared a World Heritage Site. In Saskatchwan the recent opening of the Wanuskewin Heritage Park is a superb example of a learning interpretative center.

Many themes could be used to establish "live" interpretive centers to illustrate mining, forestry, agriculture, oil and gas development, and fishing in areas across Canada. The thrust should be educational and experiential.

Experiential Tourism

Mass tourism has been the mainstay of the tourist industry in the past - a strange concoction of regimented and homogenous itineraries and encouragement of robotic participants. Tourism by the masses for the masses. It is a distance form of tourism - the tourist is always remote from the experience. A bus trip involves a look at the mountains from the bus - there is no attempt or desire to experience the mountains or become part of the mountains. Alternate tourism and especially one of its offshoots - experiential tourism attempts to close this gap. It puts the experiential tourist in the mountains or the ocean itself. It encourages the tourist to challenge and become part of the tourist attraction by hiking, trekking, canoeing, climbing, mountaineering, orienteering, skiing, or snow shoeing. Experiential tourism is not limited, however, to the natural environment. Experiential tourism can be an urban experience as part of the arts, culture, shopping, or attractions milieu. Zoos have attempted to shift from passive to more active experiences. First, by building habitat enclosures rather than cages. Secondly by introducing petting zoos, walkaround animals and a range of educational and environmental programs.

There have been many successful attempts to integrate tourism, shopping and leisure into a desired experience. This attempts to elevate shopping from the level of a chore to a desirable and sought after experience. It integrates a whole set of experiences in terms of not just a large array of shops but the architecture, lighting, entertainment, amusement and leisure. Indoor and outdoor markets such as Granville Island in Vancouver have successfully captured the experiential shopper. The consummate experiential project is probably the West Edmonton Mall, the boldest and grandest experiment in winning over the leisure or experiential tourist combining numerous shops, a vast indoor amusement park as well as a water park with artificial beach.

Extravaganzas sell! For the doubters we need only whisper "The Phantom of the Opera." Many segments of the population have a clear preference for a one time splurge in entertainment, rather than a continuous stream of events of more modest proportions. The cultural groups are slowly catching on. While many classical concerts are hard-pushed to fill 30 percent of their seats, a well balanced program

---

in an exotic setting - an extravaganza - will sell tickets in the plus-10,000 range. We have not even tapped this potential. Cultural events set in the mountains, on lakes, on paddlesteamers, on the ocean, offer large potential. Large festivals can be a magnet for tens of thousands of people with themes of jazz , country and western music, classical music, rock concerts, theatre and art,

Tourism in the future will see a decline in mass tourism and a growing interest in alternate tourism as denoted through the 5Es. Demographic changes will propel this shift as the growth in middle aged tourists with larger discretionary incomes seek out unique or customized experiences. Taste will replace crass. The middle aged are more likely to seek out eco-tours, educational tours and experiential pursuits. Frequency of trips, rather than length of trips will become a governing norm. The axis of trip length will move from multi-week to multi-day. The future tourist will have a different profile from the past. They will be older and most likely middle-age. They will be more affluent, but much more demanding of quality, value for money, service and personal experiences. They will be much more demanding of both physical and mental stimulus in their free time and will aim to combine learning and fun in the same tourist trip. The increasing, rather than decreasing, pressure on consumer's time will mean a far more discriminating and demanding tourist in terms of balancing disposable income and leisure time available. Quality tourism and quality time will become the key words for the 1990s and beyond.

New technologies will also impact tourism, particularly information technology. More sophisticated computerized systems will better match individual consumers' wants with available tourist experiences. Tourist agencies emphasizing alternate tourism will prosper. Smart cards will probably become the norm at visitor intensive locations to control visitor flows in an optimal manner and also to enhance security.

The largest developments, however, will occur in the field of interpretive experiences. Information technology will revolutionize the presentation of information at museums and other entertainment centers by literally assimilating the tourist in the experience. Opportunities abound for enriching learning experiences through interactive media and multimedia. By the successful merger of video, text, audio and animation, multimedia software will be capable of transporting us to foreign lands, take us to the real habitats of animals, fish and birds and complement our experiences at museums, zoos and parks. Simulation technology will be able to create real life experiences and thrills, without the risk themselves. All this will eventually take us into the realm of virtual reality, where using sophisticated information technology, we will be able to create real worlds and experiences in virtual reality centers. The ultimate in the final "E" - escapism.

While increasing numbers of Canadians will flock overseas, the challenge for the Canadian travel industry will be to attract larger numbers of tourists to Canada. Facilitating this will be easier in terms of exploiting the specialized "5Es," than it

---

has been in the mass tourism market. By European and Japanese standards we should be a highly competitive destination, in terms of experiences, variety, a pristine environment and low costs. Yet, historically, we have been pitiful in marketing our facilities and development of the packages to entice foreigners based on the 5Es principles and themes.

9

EDUCATION - THE GREYING OF THE GREY CELLS

A Changing World

Education will be a growth industry into the 21st Century, but the students will be a greyer hue. This will become the age of the adult continuous learner. Education will no longer be just kid's stuff!

Future success will depend on continuous improvement of knowledge and skills. Change will dictate more emphasis on adult upgrading across all facets of the job spectrum. This is not a world of education elitism, this is a world of upgrading for all. Not just professionals, but also para-professionals, technicians, the trades and semi-skilled workers.

Take the world of the car mechanic - a work environment pounded by technological refinements. Today's car is a myriad of materials including increasing plastics, composites and aluminum. The car has abundant electronics, computers and soon, automated guiding systems. It has anti-lock braking, turbochargers and no-fill batteries. Diagnostics for repairs will be carried out by expert systems and, of course, most maintenance and repair work records are fully computerized. Inventory systems are fully computerized. No longer a job of just wrenches and oily rags!

Few in the workforce today will escape the need for lifetime learning of both new skill-sets and new knowledge. We are far more demanding of our workers. Technical competence was often the only requirement in the past. I remember when I was hired straight from university in 1970 by a small Canadian geological and geochemical consulting company. Their only requirement was really my specific technical expertise in geochemistry; little else mattered. How times have changed. In most areas, today, we look for a composite skill-set, embracing one's specific technical expertise as well as one's commercial acumen and of increasing importance, one's interpersonal or relational skills. In fact, one looks at job advertisements today and one sees a ubiquitous desire to hire superman and superwoman (even though many of the senior hirers are remarkably delinquent in many of the required skills themselves).

Compounding the problem is the nature of change itself, with its inherent, built-in redundancy factor. Whether the rate of change overall is accelerating is a moot point, but certainly in many areas of high technology the half-life of knowledge is being compressed. In the "slow" 1960s it was commonly believed that the half-life of knowledge was about 15 years in most scientific and engineering fields; that is half the knowledge learned became irrelevant over a period of 15 years. Today, that half life of knowledge according to many is probably more like 5 years . . . and still declining. In many areas of computer science it may well be already as low as two years. Certainly, in the area of conventional computer software, upgrades or new products are certainly emerging bi-annually, with obvious implications regarding re-education. In reality, we probably fail to effectively differentiate between knowledge and information and it is very debatable if knowledge is accelerating as rapidly as we believe. Information is certainly proliferating - much of it hardly new, very repetitive and continuously re-packaged to give a veneer of novelty.

The New Business Of Education

Enrollments are booming everywhere in post-secondary education - universities, community colleges, vocational institutions, trade colleges and a myriad of private colleges, institutions and ad hoc courses, seminars and conferences. This at a time, when public funding of education is being constrained or even reduced. The result is rather self-evident - a future boom in private education for adults.

Adult education is yet again a fragmented market and many niche businesses will be created to meet specific consumer needs and wants. Two major segments of adult education can be delineated:

> ➢ goal-oriented, career, job and business related education;
> ➢ enrichment, personal development or pure knowledge seeking education.

There are many categories within each segment, from casual talks and seminars to full undergraduate or postgraduate degree programs.

Personal Development And Self-Fulfillment

This facet of education will experience burgeoning growth, as Canada's population ages. Beyond the age of the early- to mid-40s, educational upgrading starts to change from a goal-oriented career focus to one with more emphasis on the quest of knowledge for enrichment and personal development. It is driven more by a need to satisfy the inner-self. Emerging Canadian demographics will ensure strong growth in this facet of education into the next century. Changing attitudes towards work, leisure and the desire to achieve a balanced perspective will lead to strong growth in personal development education.

The scope of seminars, courses and conferences in this area are immense, but will focus on culture-related learning, history, archaeology, the arts, linguistics, the environment, world religions, philosophy, social issues, wellness issues and personal exploration and development. There will be a large increase in leisure and active living pursuits such as educational tours, photography, wildlife studies, hiking, adventure tours, art, music, food, wine education and gardening. Ethnicity will become a fusing rather than a division of minds and experience.

Increasingly such courses and conferences will lead to growth in rural and remote retreats and conference centres, in aesthetically appealing locations, in the mountains or by lakes or the ocean. This will blur the boundaries at times between education and tourism, many seeking a fusion of learning, mental stimulus, fun and relaxation. These centres will become loci for the rejuvenation of some remote and rural areas and will be catalysts for other local employment opportunities, such as maid services, dry cleaning, food and beverage services, tourist businesses, accommodation and specific educational or tourist attractions.

It's All In The Tongue

Communication is just that much easier if one speaks the language. Globalization of the world's economies will lead to increasing demand for linguistics. The North American Free Trade Agreement (NAFTA) will bring us closer to Mexico and the requirement to communicate in Spanish. Europe continues down the path of fuller integration, at least at the economic level, and the increasing demand for multi-lingual communications. The awakening and long dormant giant of China will likely have a compelling impact on global economics and trade flows. Learning Mandarin will be a requirement, or at least a major advantage, in doing business in China.

Linguistics education looks set to soar on three different planes. The first is due to a strong rebound in immigration to Canada with currents levels of net immigration reaching almost 200,000 immigrants annually. This is about triple the values of about one decade ago. Moreover, the composition of immigrants has changed dramatically. In the 1950s and 1960s about one third of all immigrants arrived from the United Kingdom. Today, the ethnic mix of immigrants is much more diverse, with about 75 percent being visible minorities from Asia, Africa, the Caribbean and Latin America. For many, English or French is not their first language. The immediate demands of these immigrants is rapid assimilation and this is greatly facilitated by learning of English or French as a second language. Thus, the teaching of either of these languages to recent immigrants will blossom over the next decade or so, as we ride the crest of a new immigration up-cycle.

The second boom in language training will be to meet the growing needs of globalization and Canada's need to reach out to the global growth markets. This pinpoints a need for the specific languages of high growth economies in southeast Asia, such as Japan, China, Hong Kong, Taiwan and South Korea, as well as the Latin American countries. As NAFTA expands over time to embrace other countries in Latin America, the need for Spanish (and to a more limited extent, Portuguese) will prosper.

The third boom in linguistics will be in response to increasing globalization of tourism. Canadians will travel overseas more and more. Language learning will become more desirable to achieve a better understanding of the country and its people and also facilitate the travel experience. This becomes part of the personal development and fulfillment arena.

Alternate Delivery Systems For Education

Technological advancement offers the potential of alternate delivery systems for education, especially to remote locations. While the conventional classroom environment of teacher and student will reign supreme for the foreseeable future, alternate delivery systems will encroach upon conventional systems. This will be driven by many factors, often unrelated, such as choice, flexibility, constraints on public funding for post-secondary education, declining cost of new technology and burgeoning demands for post-secondary education in an age of the education continuum.

Technology is becoming the vehicle of education choice. Audio tapes, video tapes, satellite delivery and fibre optics opens up new channels of educational programming. Interactive teleconference systems will allow further development, partially simulating a conventional teacher-student classroom relationship. Obviously, bearing in mind John Naisbitt's term of high-tech, high-touch, the future will entail a cornucopia of different delivery systems, probably best captured in the term multi-media. This will ultimately entail customizing education to the individual consumer's preferences for a particular learning medium.

Undoubtedly, the new technologies are liberating in many respects as they open up avenues of learning for previously under-privileged groups. Distance or home-based education delivery systems are ideal for certain types of clientele, for example, those living in remote communities, inmates in penitentiaries, the disabled, people with abnormal work shifts/patterns, and those preferring flexible, rather than rigid and time-defined, schedules. Distance education, in itself, is hardly new and has been practiced for many years (for example, Athabasca University at Fort McMurray and Télé Université de Montreal). New technology, however permits a whole range of new options and alternate delivery systems.

Alternate delivery systems for education will also be propelled by the large-scale expansion in student enrollments at a time of stagnant or contracting funding for many areas of post-secondary education. Escalating entry standards are being used as screening and quota devices to reject many capable students. This will inevitably lead to a growth in off-campus or "electronic education centers," based on the established regional models of Athabasca or the Télé University or a new country-wide "University of the Skies." Such a system would combine satellite communications (largely for rural and remote areas) and fibre optics (largely for inter-urban links) as well as VHF radio telephone, cellular radio and microwave technology. Even computer-assisted instruction has evolved from its early use for rote memorization and drill to more creative simulation tools, creative exercises and even artistic expression.

Alternate delivery systems will be used largely in supplemental situations to conventional teaching methods, as well as filling necessary voids in more remote locations and meeting the needs of those unable to gain entrance to conventional learning centres. Information technology will leverage the dissipation of "super teachers" to country-wide or even global audiences.

Beyond national objectives, however, distance or alternate delivery systems have a large potential as an exportable product. It is not difficult to visualize in the near future a variety of specialized international schools based in Canada, connected by interactive satellite or trans-ocean fibre optics systems to remote learners in the Third World. Such a system would be a commercial enterprise or a more meaningful application of Third World Aid. Education services could be bartered for tradable commodities produced by the Third World country. Piped-in education would be a cost effective, rapid transfer service, aimed at upgrading the educational systems in deprived Third World countries very rapidly. It could be used to market advice and expertise that we have developed in natural resources development and infrastructure development.

Distance education will permit the development of these global niches in specialized education centres within Canada. This could result in effective dissemination and leverage of Canadian expertise in areas such as natural resources development, telecommunications and agricultural biotechnology. This would include training centers in oil and gas services, energy management, mining technology, cereal and livestock production, transportation and infrastructure development. These would become magnets of global students through a combination of conventional teaching methods and off-site electronic studies.

Canada with its non-colonization past is in a perfect position to capitalize upon a role as major educator for the Third World. One can imagine specialized Global Education Centres (GECs) in Canada, dissipating education through high-tech media to an educationally thirsting Third World.

Vocational Heaven

A transformed economy is potentially vocational heaven. With the marked shift in Canada from resource and related developments to a more value creating, knowledge-intensive society, the opportunities for re-skilling are limitless. Our conventional school system can hardly be, nor should they be, geared to solely vocational training. They provide the educational platform, upon which vocational skills, knowledge and experience can be built.

The demands for vocational training in a world of emerging massive skill shifts and mismatches will be enormous. While public institutions, under funding constraints, will make valiant efforts to service these needs, reality suggests a massive development of private schools and facilities. Many of these facilities could be amendable to franchise developments, country-wide or even North American wide. Specialized franchise operations could develop in computer software tuition, management courses, linguistics and basic upgrading skills and maybe basic literacy programs. Franchised operations will co-exist with a myriad of independent operators responding to increasing demands for upgrading technical, commercial and relational skills. As the business world continues to fragment as part of business miniaturization the need for small business competency upgrading will soar.

10

RETAIL - THE AGE OF DISCERNMENT

Retail - The Age Of Discernment

Retailing in the 1990s will be a tough business. Gone are the days of solid growth in mass markets. Gone also will be the role of the departmental store, trying to be everything to all people. In their wake will develop a complex array of market fragments and niches, with well-honed market strategies.

The 1990s are bringing a new paradigm to retailing. In many areas, we are over-retailed. We are certainly over-malled, after the 1980s' construction binge. In the 1980s retail outlets increased by 50 percent as opposed to population growth of only 20 percent. The cutbacks are coming. We have also been deluged with sameness in the characterless, faceless malls and bland chains. Future growth will emphasize individualism and uniqueness or price. Polarization will occur between the large warehouse concept of retailing, the "category killers" and the refined, personalized service premium markets of the specialist niche retailer. To some extent, this will be polarization along American versus Canadian retailers.

Yet, new trends present new opportunities in the incredibly diverse world of retailing. Dual income families will become the norm and this will drive the direction of retail goods and services. Time, or lack of, will create a myriad of retailing opportunities. Home delivery of meals will increase, especially among baby-boomers with children. But, home delivery tastes will change with a growth in gourmet, exotic and more health-conscious foods. More and more people will eat out and more often. Today, over a quarter of all meals are eaten outside of the home. By the turn of the century this will be approaching half, driven by childless baby-boomers, baby-boomers with aging children and the aging of the population itself. This is the de-cocooning wave, which will follow Faith Popcorn's much over-stated cocooning wave. The restaurant business will boom, but will be intensely competitive. The trend will be towards the casual, the different and value for money. There will be room for fewer expensive, up-market restaurants. Eating out will evolve to the frequent norm, rather that the infrequent celebratory meal. Important changes will occur in the clothing sector. The big change in the 1990s will be that the world of business will go casual. Suits for men will be out, casual slacks and sweaters in. This will mean important changes for the retail menswear sector. Declining sales will characterize suits, dress shirts and ties. Stylish, elegant and higher quality casual wear will expand. The trend will be more muted and delayed among females, as they will be more reluctant to test "office tolerance" in a world still dominated by male management.

Large indoor regional malls will continue to relinquish market share to indoor market concepts, local malls, character neighbourhood streets, and older, refurbished parts of urban centres. Courtyard shopping complexes will be in. The independent retailer emphasizing quality and "high touch" will regain market share from the bland, faceless "low touch" chains. The focus on service quality will preferentially differentiate the independent retailer over the chains. In fact, the differences will be exacerbated as chains evolve to "throw-away" pools of part time labour.

The Department Store/Supermarket Blues

Indifferent service, poor inventories and wayward strategies are sowing the seeds of destruction for the "mall anchors." Both department stores and supermarkets will be the endangered species of the 1990s, as new superstores, hypermarkets and super warehouses erode their markets on the low price end of the spectrum and quality, personal service, and uniqueness of the specialist retailer erode their market share on the quality/image end. Positioning for the middle is positioning for extinction. Already a heritage institution - Woodwards - has disappeared in western Canada. Other department stores are ailing as they are battered on all sides by either low prices, better inventories and selection or better quality and better service. Similarly, supermarkets are caught in a cost- squeeze rut. Their response couldn't be worse - cut quality and reduce staff.

Department stores and supermarkets, for so long the unassailable institutions of Canada, have been caught off guard in a new world of proliferating big store formats on the one hand, and death by a thousand specialists cuts on the other. Their response has been to freeze in a time warp. Meanwhile, the giant warehouses focusing unabashedly on low service and low price are beginning to capture large chunks of market share in white goods, hardware, furniture and toys. At the other end of the spectrum, small specialty stores are offering better service, better choice, competitive pricing and a personalized touch that department stores are unable to deliver. Department stores epitomize the death spiral of a reinforcing loop of reducing costs, which reduces service, which begets more cost reduction. The department stores are plagued by high overhead costs, as well as high inventory costs from covering such a wide range of goods. Yet, they are often targets of criticism for being frequently low on stock. In addition the compartmentalization of service causes a hassle for shoppers and makes shopping time-consuming running from one department to another. Department store survival will depend on embarking on improved just-in-time inventory concepts, as well as an increasing market focus on fewer goods and services. In future, department stores may embrace the concept of a collection of microbusinesses, by contracting out various goods and services sales to independent retailers. This would result in both lower inventory and overhead costs, as well as improved customer service. The department store would cover marketing and overall administrative issues, in return for a share of profits or an over-riding royalty. This in many respects is the evolution towards a "market" setting for shopping, a trend that may become entrenched in future. Whether departmental stores can develop this concept in mall environments to create the atmosphere of the true independent "markets" now developing remains to be seen.

The 1990s will be the era of Americanization of the large format retail sector in Canada, as U.S. large stores and category killers overrun their Canadian-owned equivalents. Much of this will occur through superior service, more knowledgeable staff, more comprehensive inventories, and lower prices. Our retail sector will, as a result, evolve to a hard core of American-owned large store formats (customer-focused department stores and category killers) coexisting with a large fringe of Canadian specialty stores and franchise operations.

Supermarkets, in turn, are being buffeted by change and, in particular, the erosion in market share to huge superstores and hypermarkets. The latter offer choice, low prices, but low service. Instead of competing in their supposed areas of strength, supermarkets are trying unsuccessfully to compete on their terms. This means cost reduction reflected in poor service, declining quality of produce and slower checkouts and elimination of car service. Yet, ironically the supermarket's survival will depend on their evolution back to quality and service, as a key differentiation strategy from the low cost, bare bones warehouses and hypermarkets. The supermarkets need to return to premium quality produce and products and impeccable service for the time-constrained consumer.

Supermarkets have an unparalleled opportunity to develop a winning survival strategy. This means redesigning the checkout bottleneck and offering electronic shopping services with home delivery. Time is at a premium for the new world of dual income families - few regard grocery shopping as quality time or productive leisure time. If supermarkets fail to fill this void, direct marketing companies using videotex systems with interactive computers or cable television monitors will dominate this emerging market segment. Failure of supermarkets to move into ordering and delivery systems will mean extinction in face of very competitive, but low service superstores or rise of direct marketing services. Another form of differentiation for supermarkets is to offer the consumer a shopping experience. This could span the field from demonstrations on food preparation, product manufacture, videos and entertainment.

Pseudo-customization

True individualization comes at a price and is usually restricted to the up-market specialty retailers. This means lots of attention, lots of time and maybe personal visits to the customer's home. It is a growing market, yes, but, by definition, hardly a mass market.

In a world of evolving technology, however, the best of both worlds can be achieved at competitive prices. This is the world of Pseudo-Customization, where technology produces customization for mass markets. This has evolved through the facilitating nature of new, automated manufacturing technologies employing advanced forms of information technology. These are the flexible manufacturing facilities of modern plants, with computer-assisted manufacturing and design, statistical process control, and electronic data interchange. Pseudo-customization, through information technology, offers infinite variety at prices with mass appeal.

Pseudo-customization offers endless possibilities for the personalization of goods and services. High-tech flexible production lines can produce infinite variety in automobiles, motorcycles, bicycles, computers and even food products such as soups, pastas, cereals and soft drinks.

Information services are very amenable to pseudo-customization such as personalized promotion literature, personalized databases, executive briefing and scanning services. Telephone services through the talking yellow pages offers personalized information for a wide variety of tastes. Even the Karoake bar offers personalized singing for the masses.

Future technology via the home entertainment systems will offer unparalleled opportunities for personalizing entertainment on a mass basis. We will be able to put together our own combinations of music, programming, education tapes and sporting events (all without advertisements).

The largest growth in the pseudo-customization market is the superb choice of products available at the category killer stores. These stores have carved out themselves a unique sleight of hand of both mass service and mass customization.

At the other end of the spectrum are an array of largely independent retailers playing on personalized or individualized services in well-defined niche markets. Prices are undoubtedly higher, but the customer finds compensation in the specialized products or services combined with caring, personalized service. At these stores, unlike the category killers one is not just a number. These stores will focus on products that are different, maybe a little more exotic, more design-oriented and better quality. They cater to the consumer seeking quality, design, and uniqueness.

This will range from the specialized kitchenware store to the specialist card store to the specialized coffee shop with a unique atmosphere and comraderie.

Franchise Futures

Expanding opportunities in franchising will co-exist with the true independent retailer. The demands for predictability, consistency and reliability will always be a preference for an important segment of the population. The franchise is the retailers' half-way house. It has an element of predictability and quality assurance that certain consumers require, yet it has the independent business person's stamp of individuality. It, therefore, bridges the gap between the bland chains and the "unknown" aspect of the true independent retailer.

Franchising will expand as the fragmentation of markets increasingly verges towards a smaller denomination. Franchising is part and parcel of the inevitable miniaturization of business and growth in para-entrepreneurship. It satisfies the desires to run one's own business, but part of the risk is absorbed by a proven track record of the franchisor. Yet, it gives the franchisee all the attributes of running their own business and a sense of controlling their own destiny.

Franchises will continue to develop rapidly, as the consumer seeks out guaranteed quality and service at reasonable prices. Their ability to attract more committed employees will lever their advantages over departmental stores and chains. The franchisees will have the ability to put their stamp of individuality on a franchise. There are countless new opportunities for franchise ideas in both products and services.

The future environment is especially ripe, however, for an explosion of new franchise ideas in personal services. This is true in both the trades and professional services, where highly variable quality and service creates the perfect vehicle for franchising. A solid foundation of business planning, proven ventures and top notch training will also render financing such ventures easier than independent businesses. But, the delivery of a different product will allow both franchises and the completely independent businesses to prosper as they cater to different market segments concurrently.

Opportunity Futures - Franchises

- Gourmet Coffee Houses/Tea Houses
  (the "new" meeting places in the "new" economy)
- Fresh Pasta Outlets
- Fitness Centres
- Brew Pubs
- The Trades - Electricians/Plumbers/Auto Mechanics/Tilers
- Fresh Juice Bars
- Exotic Salad Bars
- Vegetarian Bistros
- Music Lessons
- Acupuncture Clinics
- Stress Consultants/Clinics
- Tutorial Services
- Financial Planning Centres
- Day Care Centres
- Para-Legal Divorce Centres
- Nursing Homes
- Home Entertainment Installations
- Accounting "Stores"
- Legal "Stores"
- Wine Bars
- Private Wine Stores
- Energy Management Services
- Pet Kennels/Care
- Veterinary Clinics
- Landscaping Services
- Home Renovations
- Singles Matching Services
- Senior's Leisure Centres
- Window - Cleaning Services
- Diagnostic Medical Clinics

Future Retail Tangents

The retail industry will, in many respects, parallel trends in the rest of the economy. That means spinning off separate tangents with well-defined market fragments, strategic niches and very focused market strategies. Knowing where one fits will be critical to survival - a fuzzy strategy and attempting to be all things to all people will be a dangerous trend to extinction.

Five major retail tangents will emerge:

1. **The Bottom Feeders** will cater to the price conscious consumer willing to forego convenience and service. It is the self-serve supermarkets, the warehouses and the low-cost department stores. Price, low that is, will be the only driver for this market.

2. **The Mass Customiser** will combine competitive prices with vast selections, but only in a limited product range. This group includes the "category killers" and a lot of franchise operators. Service and quality must be excellent, but not necessarily exceptionally personalized.

3. **The Experiental Shopper** is the professional shopper, the one turned on continuously by the shopping experience. They prefer the malls, where there is abundant choice and variety of stores. But, they will be expecting a lot more from malls or there will be continuing leakage of experiental shoppers to markets, neighbourhood shopping streets and new courtyard and strip mall complexes.

4. **The Arm-Chair Shopper** is the one who despises shopping. They want electronic shopping preferably with delivery service. This is as yet an untapped market, which will be the growth sector as telecommunication networks penetrate the home. Home-select, home-order and delivery to the door will be the expectation for this market segment. Selection and service will be critical.

5. **The Personalized Retailer** will be the niche specialist offering the specific, high quality products, and exceptional personalized service. Prices must be broadly competitive, but are not critical. With the personalized retailer, the customer, as an individual, is everything.

11

PERSONAL SERVICES -
TIME DEARTH

The Paradox of Time

Time has become in many respects, the new currency of the 1990s. Many futurists have long preached the coming age of leisure. Yet, in the 1990s we all seem even more time constrained. What really explains this apparent paradox? I think that it all lies in the statistics - maybe they don't lie, just distort the truth. There is no doubt that over the last several decades the length of the official work week has declined substantially, though little, if any, in the last decade or so. Therefore, defining leisure as simply the residual part of the day, it is indisputable that leisure time has increased.

This simple model, however, does not reflect reality. It ignores the fact that many salaried employees, particularly in the insecure 1990s, work well beyond the "official" work week. Many take substantial work home. Many more moonlight at a second job or are part of the rapidly growing underground economy. Thus, official statistics significantly understate work and overstate the trend to increasing leisure time.

Perhaps the major controversy, though, is the definition of the word leisure. Most of us would dispute that the residual part of the day, after work, is truly leisure. For many the joys of travel to work is not leisure. The joys of housework, now invariably done on top of a regular job, does not constitute leisure to many of us. Thus, what we are really defining is the amount of discretionary time available for us to pursue our true interests or leisure pursuits. There is little doubt that this has declined in our modern society and continues to decline. The pressures of increasing length of commutes, dual income families, moonlighting and combo-jobs has contracted our pure discretionary leisure time. This is the catalyst for a booming personal services sector in the 1990s and beyond.

Time will be the scarce commodity as we enter the 21st century. Business ideas driven by this one simple factor will invariably reap dividends. Much has indeed changed and is still changing to siphon off leisure time. Undoubtedly, the biggest social change is the new preponderant work structure of dual income families, and in the 25-45 year old age group the female participation rate already approaches that of males. In addition, in many large urban centres commuting times are getting longer, people are working longer hours (often propelled by concern for their jobs) plus very flexible working patterns. Split shifts are now commonplace and evening and Sunday work are becoming a social norm. Not only is there a crunch on leisure time per se, there is a problem of families getting congruent and coincident leisure time. It is, no longer far fetched that families will have to make appointments to see each other!

According to Juliet Schor in her book "The Overworked American," over the past twenty years fully employed people have increased their time at work (both in the office and home) by as much as an extra month a year. We are rapidly becoming an overworked, overextended and increasingly stressed out breed of workers. And we thought it was just the Japanese!

Time dearth will become the issue of the 1990s and beyond - it will become the scourge of the consumer. After all, one factor is inextricably fixed - there are only 24 hours in a day!

Of course, the squeeze on time spins off a whole set of business opportunities. Retailing attributes must change to accommodate stress-laden, weary, full time workers. This will demand rapid service, flexible hours, comprehensive selection, good inventories, optional delivery systems (self service, full service, advisory services), high value for money and convenience. More and more opportunities will arise for the substitution of consumer time and labour by business. Increasingly, the time laden consumer will trade time for money outlays. The following are some key business opportunities.

Grocery Shopping

It is too time consuming, too busy and too stressful for working partners. The 1990s will see a return of an old village concept - home delivery. Isn't it ironic how many ideas go full cycle? A combination of time constraints, opportunity and technology will fill the void. The consumer will be able to bring up the shopping list on the home computer with regular items already highlighted. Additions and deletions will be made in a few minutes and via the modem, the completed shopping list is electronically sent to the local supermarket or superstore. Delivery of the basket of goods will be made at the consumer's convenience - at a price!

Professionals

It is the irony of modern "democracy" that professionals expect trades people and the retail sector to be on call on a virtual 24 hour basis BUT us professionals...

I am sorry, but the luxury of 9 to 5 working hours for many professionals is doomed. Wake up doctors, dentists, lawyers, and accountants, the world is calling and not 9 to 5 (except on a Saturday and Sunday), but evenings as well. The enterprising few are emerging from the woodwork and setting the new convenience standard for the 1990s. Those leading the way will see their business thrive, while the laggards will see a shrinking client base. One result of this requirement for extended hours will be more partnerships and professional pooling, in order to share the burden of longer and more irregular hours. Professional franchises will develop to better serve clients and offer nation-wide convenience of time and services.

Home Services

The explosion in contracting out home chores will continue. Housecleaning, house painting, window cleaning, snow-shoveling, and landscaping/gardening, the live-in housekeeper/au pair will all flourish in the 1990s. Only sex and sleep will escape replacement labour! Increasing concerns on security will lead to a bigger role for house-sitters, as well as pet-sitters. Pets will be as popular as ever, but time dearth will often preclude Fido's walk. Enter the new personal service of walking other people's dogs.

Leisure Chauffeurs

More valuable time is committed to nuisance driving to the library, dry cleaners, trips for children's cultural lessons and sports. People will start contracting out these activities to leisure chauffeurs, booked on a block of time per month. This will open up new untapped markets for taxi drivers with a guaranteed monthly income.

Electronic Gadgetry Set-Up

We have probably all experienced the frustrations of bringing home the latest hot electronic product, only to be foiled for hours in setting it up. Hooking up VCRs with their scramblers, decoders, cable systems, and other miscellaneous gizmos ends up being the non-handyperson's nightmare. Stereo equipment and even loading software programs on computers can be equally formidable. Customer services in these areas is sorely lacking and seems to stop at the door of the store. In the future world of entertainment centres and rooms with all these wonderful electronic products interlinked, such post-sale services will be mandatory. For most of us, precious time is more productively and less frustratingly spent elsewhere with less stress.

PART IV

THE FUTURE WORKPLACE

12

ORGANIZATIONAL CHANGE

"Hey, size works against excellence"
Bill Gates, Microsoft Corp.

Business Miniaturization

Business Goes to the Shrink

Just like the world of computers, where the microcomputer is replacing mainframe applications, the world of business is going small. Fragmentation of markets and demand has its parallels on the supply side with declining big business, and a proliferation of the micro-provider of goods and services. This trend is unstoppable in today's world of intense competition, wide availability of resources and information, deregulation of monopolistic industries and instant globalization. This environment favours the flexible, efficient, effective, innovative and the fast; in short, micro-business.

The future will be continuing loss of market share by many mega-business in many sectors of the domestic Canadian economy at the expense of micro-business. There is a dynamic at work here, however, as there is an irresistible urge by many micro-businesses to become big. This either leads to the eventual self destruction of the business, as inefficiencies emerge and bureaucracy grows or new organization structures evolve that effectively simulate small business operations. In this context the quotation by Bill Gates that starts this section on micro-business is revealing. Microsoft Corp. is now a large business. How it operates in the future and how it retains its dynamism and entrepreneurial attributes in an expansive structure will be interesting. One suspects the company will either self-destruct under its own weight or it evolves to a cellular structure which retains small business norms.

The Competition Whirlwind

Nothing works like competition. Competition is the fuel for consumers, but the bane of big business. Market domination through monopoly, market discipline, cartelization or regulation has been good news for big business. But when the competition gets tough, the big go on a diet, or disappear. It is not difficult to be big and profitable as a monopolist (De Beers in diamonds), or in existing or formerly cartelized businesses (oil companies and airlines), or in markets where oligopolies create rigid market discipline (major pharmaceutical companies). Regulated industries are usually paragons of inefficiency and profitability. Many industries fit in this category in Canada including telephone companies, pipeline companies, electric and gas utilities. Regulated by boards totally divorced from economic realities, most of these companies in today's very competitive markets have watched their real returns on investment soar, as inflation has receded. Deregulation would indeed be the enemy for these organizations, but a wonderful salvation for the consumer. For those of a doubting disposition we need only think of the large declines in air fares and the significant declines in long distance telephone calls as part of a recent surge in deregulation.

As governments learn about the inefficiencies, and high costs of monopolies, cartelized and regulated markets, fragmentation of industries will lead to a surge in competitive forces. The swift-moving small companies thrive on low costs, innovation and new ideas, in contrast to the slow lumbering giants fattened by years of regulated or protected markets.

Scale economies alone bestowed significant advantages to large corporations, catering to mass markets, buoyant economic growth and a reasonably predictable consumer. Technological developments in manufacturing, logistics, marketing and information technology have changed our focus, however, from economies of scale to economies of scope. Economic growth is less predictable and the consumer is very fickle. In many areas of the economy, fads have replaced trends. Flexibility, therefore, is the new buzzword for the new economy, a trait strongly favouring small over big business.

Weaned on growth, scale economies and centralized structures, big corporations and governments at all levels allowed the development of bloated organization superstructures. Management proliferated, especially middle management with its proclivity to create non-productive work. Middle management essentially carved out a non-function - politely called coordination - whereby their subordinates did the work and executives made the decisions. Big corporations are now addressing the problem, while governments at all levels have yet to bite the bullet, with the exorcism still to come.

The Small White Sharks

The inventiveness and innovation of humans is limitless, given the right environment. Big business is hardly conductive to this type of thinking, where conventional, "toe-the line thinking" is virtually mandated. "Shoot the messenger" has long been the creed at many large corporations. Not surprisingly, therefore, small is leading the revolution in many industry sectors and causing massive upheavals of industry structure.

As Ken Iverson of Nucor Corporation, a U.S. steel mini-mill said: "Technology is taking the scale out of everything." The new information technologies reduce the optimal size of business and make a mockery of scale economies. Economies of scope through marketing alliances, partners or unique distributorships or channels, allow the small to thrive at the expense of the big. As we move to more niche products and individualized markets, scale becomes increasingly redundant in the world of knowledge-intensive, value creating production. Fragmentation spurns big and spurs small.

Numerous examples abound of small leading big in many industry sectors and even in frontier technologies. It was Apple Corp. through its advanced icons and windows principles that transformed computers and virtually invented the phrase "user-friendly." Apple gave birth to the revolutionary concept of desktop publishing. IBM took years to catch up. It was upstart, Microsoft Corp. that revolutionized the software business to put it into its dominant position today. Even in the ultra-sophisticated scientific world of biotechnology, breakthroughs are emanating from the small, rather than the pharmaceutical behemoths. Genentech, based in California, first produced the blockbuster synthetic human insulin followed by Activase which literally can stop cardiac seizures in progress. Biomira Inc., based at Edmonton, Alberta, is probably the leading Canadian biotechnology company. Their leading product, Theratape, is now undergoing phase two trials and is aimed at stimulating the body's immune system to respond to a host of cancers.

Steel technology is being revolutionized by the small, mini-mills. Nucor Inc. has developed and commercialized the first application of thin-slab, continuous casting process. This now permits the scrap-based mini-mills to compete head-on in the flat products markets, previously the sole preserve of the large, integrated steel companies.

The electric utility industry is now being impacted by new cogeneration or independent power plants, almost always spearheaded by small entrepreneurial developers. These plants are smaller, often pre-fabricated at assembly plants, produce cheaper electricity and have small lead times. They are ideal for installing capacity incrementally thus reducing the risk of inaccurate demand forecasts. They could also serve as the catalyst for a future decentralized power generation sector.

Micro-business will be characterized by rapid adaptability. The quick, fleet-footed ability to move on from saturated markets to new ventures is a continuous process of renewal and regeneration. This will be a world of niche creation and increasingly global niches. This will mean continuously innovating and differentiating goods and services. The fickleness and unlimited tastes and wants of consumers favour micro-business over macro-business. Scale economies are being subordinated to economies of scope, fragmentation and uniqueness. Focused individualization of products and services will become the new buzz word for the late 1990s. The great difficulty in separating fad from trend favours the micro-business, which will tend to get in early in contrast to larger entities that get in late and leave late.

In many respects this is the worst of worlds for big business. Used to competition from a limited number of visible large companies, large business is now vulnerable to the multi-pronged attack by a myriad of micro raiders. Micro-business will pick away markets from all sides - they will move in fast, lack visibility and individually be too small to worry about. But, in aggregate, their impact will be devastating - creating instability, uncertainty, pricing/margin pressures and loss of market share (and therefore scale) for the business Goliaths. It becomes death by a thousand nips!

The Quality/Customer Service Dilemma

No area favours micro-business over big business more than quality and customer service. In terms of big business, never has there been so much talk and so much written about as customer service, and never has there been, in reality, so little delivered. Intensive downsizing and customer service hardly go hand in hand, and predictably the contraction in staff has led to reduced customer service by most large organizations. It never ceases to amaze me that this reinforcing loop of cost cutting, leading to reduced service, leading to reduced product/service demand, leading to more cost cutting, has not been recognized or discussed by the management community. It is in many areas literally a death spiral. The trail of corporate debris is there for all to see - Woodwards, Birks, Simpsons, Massey-Ferguson, Algoma Steel, Novatel and various trust companies.

One only has to observe the shrinking role of department stores to see the death spiral at work. Cost cutting has reduced service staff to such an extent that in one of our major department stores the store is thinking of providing binoculars (and a reward) at the door to aid in tracking down a sales clerk! As service worsens, more clients drift to the boutiques, specialists or mass merchandisers; sales decline, unit costs go up and the cost cutting resumes. The demise of the Woodward's departmental store is a precursor for other failures as micro-business continues to undermine the retail Goliaths, through focus, customer service and personalized attention.

Customer service is purely a deliverable, as micro-business recognizes. It is not words, visions, mandates, plans and manuals - that is bureaucracy or as Robert Reich calls it "paper entrepreneuralism." Big companies will never deliver on customer focus until the writing diarrhea ceases and action begins. Big corporations still persist in the illusion that feeding information to the corporate monster must always take precedence over serving its customers - an insult to their customers and a further contribution to the death spiral. Meanwhile, small business focuses on action not words, plans and manuals, and really do believe and act as if the customer is number one.

The Corporate Monolith - Evolution or Devolution

The large organization as we know it has two choices - change or die. Many models have been suggested for the future monolith. Most models agree that flexibility and versatility in some form are critical to the survival of large organizations. In a rapidly changing and unpredictable business world, large organizations, especially at the head office level, have been miserable failures in the 1980s and early 1990s. Bureaucracy, politics, power struggles and empire building have reduced many to rubble - inefficient, ineffective, petrified by uncertainty and divorced from a sense of business reality.

In many cases, large organizations have attempted to supplant rigid hierarchical structures by flexible teams. While the team concept has reaped many benefits at the factory and manufacturing level, it has run into insurmountable obstacles in the radically different and more complex world of the white collar head office. In many cases, an ineffective hierarchical system has been replaced by an equally bureaucratic and smothering proliferation of teams. Going to the washroom seems to be the sole activity remaining sacrosanct from a team (for how much longer?). In turn, process has gained domination over business and rather than getting closer to the customer most organizations are now farther removed. Never have big organizations talked so much about the customer, and done so little.

The 1980s was the era of empowerment, teams, total quality management, and business process re-engineering. These were the buzzwords of the 1980s. There is little doubt that many of these concepts resulted in significant changes in industrial practices. This has been especially true in the manufacturing environment, at the factory face. The use of teams to produce and assemble many basic manufacturing products has had significant positive impacts on worker productivity and morale. Perhaps, foremost, it has humanized the production line and has undoubtedly lead to marked increases in employee dedication and product quality. It has created a new mindset - the expectation of getting it right the first time, without the costly process of rework and rejects. It has had the effect of restoring pride within the employees working on the factory floor. It has also leveraged the latent experience and contribution of all workers, by involving them in the work process. At the level of the plant, significant progress and achievements have been made in terms of increasing the productivity, product quality and the quality of the workplace itself. Part of this has involved automating those components of the job function, that are clearly better done by machines and robotics. In many respects, robotics are best employed in DDT (like the banned insecticide) applications - dirty, dangerous and tedious jobs. This then frees up the workforce talent for more skilled, innovative and challenging job roles. We will talk later about how this is leading to a challenging skill mismatch in the manufacturing environment.

We can look back with some pride to the evolution of the factory from a control-oriented, production line to a more flexible, creative and team-oriented assembly process. This has not been without its employment implications, with much more to come in the 1990s. Undoubtedly, it will mean increased job shedding and a shift from unskilled or semi-skilled work requirements to more skilled work requirements - a retraining challenge of mega-proportions.

Applying all the new concepts (Edward Deming would argue that they are hardly new, just neglected!) to the manufacturing process has had largely positive results. Problems have arisen, however, taking these processes and trying to apply them to the infinitely more complex, head office environments of large corporations (and their public sector equivalents). We are now dealing with professional and clerical staff in an ill-defined environment, infinitely more diffuse than simply manufacturing a product. We are in some cases dealing with functions that have a clear objective - marketing, sales, accounting and legal advice. But, we also have a myriad of paper entrepreneurs as Robert Reich called them, with much more vague functions and objectives. We have planners, schedulers, logistics coordinators, human resource specialists, organization effectiveness experts, information technology coordinators and many more.

Above all, measuring output is virtually impossible in the bureaucracies of large corporations and the public sector. Perhaps the only measure is paper created or trees destroyed! How does one quantify the contributions of a strategic planner, an organizational effectiveness expert, and an information technology coordinator? Blindly applying total quality management principles to this environment is clearly not going to work. In most cases that I have observed, they have been unmitigated disasters, resulting in an explosion of teams, process, human resource experts and worst of all, a proliferation in dead trees! Business process re-engineering is yet another excuse to unleash a bunch of process bureaucrats onto an already sick system. Process people are, by definition, bureaucrats and lack the very qualities of simplicity, innovation and entrepreneurship really required by large organizations. It never ceases to amaze me how these people can constantly produce meaningless convoluted flow charts, word-smith and rework documents ad nauseum and engage in endless vacuous philosophical debates on roles, responsibilities and boundary conditions. Even worse, the release of that ultimate monstrosity - the job description. The message is clear - either this bureaucratic gobbledygook goes or the large organization will fall in its wake.

Revamping the Corporate Behemoth

Bureaucracy and centralization spell the death-knell to new ideas, innovation, risk-taking and economic efficiency. Large organizations invariably develop bureaucratic and centralized infrastructures, and in this respect large corporations and government bureaucracies differ only in degree.

The successful large organization of the future, and by definition the long term survivors, will have four basic characteristics - they will be organic, they will reduce complexity, they will be segregated into small, informal units and they will be flexible. In this book, the model proposed is one of **"the amoeboid colony."** This is a fusion of two essential ingredients - multi-celling and the amoeba. To be successful, big business must try to emulate small business through disaggregation into "cells" of smaller business units. Each of these cells essentially takes on the form of the uni-celled, flexible amoeba, constantly adjusting to a changing business environment. Both the ideas of multi-celling and amoeba are metaphors for simplicity. Large organizations do not need complexity - that has been their downfall. With complexity comes process and bureaucracy, the sure death-knell of any organization. Complexity does not offer insight into uncertainty.

Multi-celling is a highly decentralized, self-directed structure, whereby big business consists essentially of an array of small businesses. But, each cell is in itself a paragon of flexibility. It does not, like our past organizational models, emphasize structure, rigidity and a languid response time to changing business conditions. Our new mental model needs to evolve from the static to the dynamic and from the inanimate to the animate.

Organizations are not static boxes and job descriptions, but living and breathing organisms. It is interesting that organizations and organisms have the same root derivative - have we been slow in recognizing this? Thus the second key analogy is that each organizational cell corresponds to the simplest form of life - the humble, uni-celled amoeba.

The Amoeboid Colony

In their book "Biology," authors William Smallwood and Peter Alexander describe an amoeba thus: "The genus amoeba is a formless creature within the phylum Sarcodina. They have often been called blobs of jelly. Amoebas have no covering outside their plasma membrane. They are **simple, flexible**, and **constantly change** their shape." Amoebas have bulges for locomotion called pseudopodia. The bulge

---

The Future Workplace

grows larger as more endoplasm flows into it. Successive pseudopodia are formed as endoplasm retracts from earlier ones which basically dissolve. Each cell of a large organization corresponds to an individual amoeba - a single, flexible, profit cell. The total organization comprises many individual amoebas in the form of an Amoeboid colony.

The Amoeba analogy produces an elegant model for the future organization. First of all we need to learn the merits of smallness and simplicity. Large, complex head offices do not work - they breed the wrong type of resources. Secondly, an organization needs to be continuously changing and adapting, but slowly and deliberately, not through periodic revolutions and palace revolts. Thirdly, the pseudopodia represent flexibility and dynamism as resources and talent can be continuously redeployed to the highest priority issues. As one issue or topic shrinks in significance, the flow of resources contracts and flows to the next pseudopodia priority. The nerve centre of the cell is now the nucleus - this is the visionary, inspirational and innovative core or team of the business cell. This core team is not a functional, but a multi-disciplinary leadership executive team. They represent the energy of the cell unit constantly challenging and re-energizing the organization to improve, excel and innovate, within its specific business.

Thus, the large organization now consists of a series of amoeba business units, networked within an amoeboid colony. One of the amoeboid cells will be the small coordination unit for the whole amoeboid colony - this is the core corporate multi-disciplinary leadership team. This team consists of individuals with the broad conceptual skills needed to assess future business attractiveness. They are the visionaries, who ultimately must decide on the allocation of investment funds leading to expansion or contraction of individual amoeboid cells, or creation of new business cells. They are leaders for the organization, not functional specialists.

Each amoeboid cell will consist of top-notch specialists for competitive edge and a much larger number of "integrated generalists." The latter will be the well qualified, generally multi-disciplinary professionals, who will provide the organization with its flexibility. These integrated generalists will be the mobile pseudopodia moving from one high priority task to the next - the physical environment, customer focus, motivation, profitability, creative financial options, new business development, acquisitions and divestitures. These integrated generalists will be high performing individuals generally qualified in both technical and commercial disciplines. The number of true specialists will be much more limited and will occur in the areas of a corporation's true competitive advantage such as polymer chemistry, geophysics, process technology and information technology. Flexibility is also enhanced by redeploying resources between individualized cells. In many respects, these business and organizational cells have no boundaries or at the very least have very fuzzy, ill-defined boundaries.

In an attempt to keep organizations to a manageable level and maximize flexibility, contracting out will become standard practice for many functions. Specialty work or peaking work will be handled through preferred contractor alliances. Other lower quality peak work will be handled through casual labour. These will be the satellite staffing services - the growth industry of the future, where essentially small business contractors increasingly siphon off work from the large organizations.

For the core employees remaining in the Amoeboid colony, the work environment is radically different to today's hierarchical, control-oriented organizations. The new organization is highly flexible, emphasizing personalized management of the individual. It addresses one of the major deficiencies of the modern organization, which is motivating a mass of peaked baby-boomers. In the new lean organizations, firstly there are less people, but also the concept of promotion and career development is radically re-defined. The concept of promotion assumes a lateral, as well as an upward, dimension, whereby resources are constantly redeployed to offer individual employees a challenging and fulfilling work environment on an on-going basis. The learning organization provides an environment of continuous learning for employees.

In effect, in this paradigm shift for large organizations their success lie in their ability to act like small business. Each cell is essentially a small business networked within an amoeboid colony. It remains simple, flexible and very responsive to changing business conditions.

The largest measure of control is maintained when multi-celling results in the development of totally decentralized, highly empowered operating business cells. The central core of such an entity is solely the executive management and a small administrative corps. The executive focus on what should be their pre-occupation - strategy, not operating the business. In Canada, probably an evolutionary model for this type of structure is CAE Ltd., the diversified conglomerate operating in four primary markets - military and space (54 percent), commercial/industrial (26 percent), industrial products (9 percent) and other aerospace and electronic (11 percent). CAE is totally decentralized. Its total worker complement is 9500 employees worldwide, but its head office has only 17 people. Strangely enough, this successful structure is hardly new and was implemented in the 1960s. Success cannot be questioned. The company has weathered recessions, substantial restructuring in many of its business lines, but has remained persistently profitable. Moreover, its decentralized structure has catalyzed innovation. CAE has captured about 75 per cent of the combined market for full flight simulators and flight training devices. Recently, CAE signed an agreement with the University of Ottawa Heart Institute to manufacture the world's first permanent artificial heart. Unlike many rigid, centralized organizations, CAE is not business-idea poor, but has a plethora of rich ideas under evaluation.

A second alternative form of multi-celling is basically the franchise. In this model, the franchiser basically creates and emulates innumerable cells of individual entrepreneurs. To all intents and purposes, these individuals act and are small business, but with corporate umbrella constraints and guidelines. The franchiser establishes a set of operating guidelines to ensure quality, ease of recognition, product type/range and advertising. The breadth of control varies extensively according to the franchiser. Some even dictate building designs and colour, while others encourage individualization, except on product or service type and quality. Franchising will continue to prosper, and will in particular enter new areas where inconsistency in quality and unpredictability of product and service delivery is rampant. Franchising is small business dressed in a veil of big business.

The third form of multi-celling is the new wave of contracting out. Disenchantment with centralized bureaucracies in large organizations, both private and public, is leading to the 1990s tide. The philosophy of big business is becoming, if you can't beat them, join them. This is the trend to contraction of big organizations to a critical mass core, presumably containing the crucial distinctive competencies, which identify the organization's competitive advantage. Allied services needed to run the organization are more effectively off-loaded to specialists or small business, capable of meeting these service needs at lower cost, higher quality and more efficiently. In effect, this is a continuing shift of jobs from big business to small business. It is not truly downsizing in an aggregate economic sense, as the loss of big business jobs are, at least party, offset by job creation in small business activities in the form of satellite groups of contract workers and a floating fringe of temporary peakers.

The next major trend will be a massive shift in government services to outsourcing. In turn, many government services will be financed on a user-pay concept rather than through general taxation. Political ideology will essentially be irrelevant to this trend. Government debt loads are now so onerous that any future government, irrespective of political hue, will be compelled to slash costs in many areas to preserve essential services such as education, health and basic welfare support. Cuts will start at the federal level and cascade down to the municipal level. Municipal spending is where government and the taxpayer really meet and this is where the accountability gap will be closed. Contracting out services will be the growth industry at the municipal level of government, as we head into the twenty-first century. Small business will prosper in response.

The Micro-Swell

Canada's future economic growth will come almost exclusively from the development of a tidal wave of entrepreneurial micro-business. These businesses will best encapsulate the key characteristics for survival as we enter the third millennium - idea-rich, innovative, flexible, fleet of foot, change-oriented and truly customer-focused. Entrepreneurial instincts will dominate. Bureaucracy in any form, including the latest business wonder-fad, will be anathema. Only large organizations actually buy into these miracle fads and spin doctors.

Big business will become shrinking employers, partly because they occupy the contracting parts of the economy, and partly due to evolution to multi-celling enclaves. The world of franchising and contracting out will proliferate. The cozy world of governments will be turned upside down, leading to a further thrust for small, independent business. The future world of employment will see an expanding majority of Canadians working in micro-business enterprises.

This, in turn, will lead to a metamorphosis in employment norms and attitudes. There will be a dramatic erosion of safe havens of employment, and little job security. For many it will mean the days of being cared for from cradle to grave by the big corporation and various governments will be a thing of the past.

Employees will become truly empowered in terms of individual responsibility for their future and financial security. In short, it means swelling numbers of employees looking after their own health-care and insurance payments. Employees will need to plan their own financial futures and retirement funds. Nothing new for those in many small businesses today, but very novel for those used to the larger public sector and private sector organizations.

Global Niche

Globalization of business was the buzzword of the 1980s. Everyone spouted the word, nobody defined it and there was an inherent belief everyone knew what it meant. I suspect few really knew what it meant, hence the difficulty in ever finding a definition. Certainly Canada or any multi-national organizations did not discover globalization in the 1980s, as both country and organizations have been global in scope for many decades.

The real difference in today's world is that modern globalization has broadened the span of participation to small enterprises. Pre-1980s the only global enterprises were the giant, multi-national organizations, that most people thought would grow and dominate world trade. In the 1980s, however, many changes occurred through technology, telecommunications, transportation and financial markets, that effectively made the world a lot smaller. Marshall McLuhan's term "global village" captures the sentiment perfectly.

The new world of globalization is indeed a smaller place. Information is traded in bulk around the world, in nano-seconds. Global financial markets which were formerly isolated enclaves, now react to money or financial moves in other markets on a daily basis. Reaction time now, through information technology, is virtually instantaneous. Information once the covetous preserve of multi-national corporations

---

is now widely available to all. Now the small business can truly create global niche markets for their business. An array of mechanisms can be set up including direct communication by an array of telecommunication devices including satellites, fax and teleconferencing. Small companies can create global partnerships, strategic alliances or promote their products and services through a variety of low cost information technology channels.

Global marketing is no longer size dependent. Economies of scope have even penetrated the world of global trade and marketing. This has given a global impetus to business miniaturization.

Beyond Empowerment to Individualized Management

Corporations have already attempted to redefine the boundaries between managers and workers. Empowering workers to take more control and decision-making has clearly benefited overall performance in many organizations. This has been particularly well-demonstrated in the manufacturing sector on the factory floor. But, in our drive for extremes, we must recognize that there are degrees of empowerment. Moreover, different workers have different thresholds for empowerment. In correcting the control-numbing style of the old paradigm, we must be wary of not swinging too far to a new paradigm of complete empowerment. Workers tolerance for empowerment is a spectrum - too much will be as counterproductive as too little.

There is, thus, a world beyond empowerment to individualized management. We must recognize that there is no one organization practice or culture, but shades of different norms. It is not a case of pure control-oriented versus empowered structures, but elements of both. Within the Amoeboid organization model will develop a spectrum of cultures and styles - different strokes for different folks! The flaw with empowerment is the universality of the concept and its thrust of overriding the needs of the individual.

Performance and productivity can only be maximized by managing people as individuals, specifically catering to their whims, idiosyncrasies and individual skill-sets. Some individuals need and want more direction and control than others. Heresies of heresies but some workers do **not** want to be empowered and their performance will be no less commendable than their empowered counterparts. Some individuals actually prefer a directed and well-defined structure in which to operate. Individualized management is the only way to maximize the individual's contribution to the organization. By definition, this also leads into the need for increasing flexibility on remuneration and benefit schemes. Tweaking the right levers for an individual will produce surprising increases in motivation, productivity and performance. The management of individuals and reward/benefit systems will be increasingly personalized. A la carte will replace table d'hôte in the world of the workplace and employment.

13

THE FUTURE JOB MARKET

The Reformation and Jobs

This book has focused on the significant structural changes occurring within the Canadian economy. Our economy is being metamorphosed before our very eyes. As we leap from the old economic solitude to the new, job patterns will undergo a similar metamorphosis.

It is indeed tragic today that career counseling takes such a static view of economic change. The younger generation is being misinformed and mislead in terms of future job trends. Career counseling in the school system is especially unenlightened in the face of massive job dislocation. In this case, the past is not a good indicator for the future. It is not overstating the fact that a whole suite of jobs is disappearing, while brand new jobs are being created as the agents provocateurs wreak employment havoc.

Many of our resource and basic manufacturing industries have entered a period of inevitable decline, elimination or, at best, stagnation. We are rapidly evolving from a resource and basic processing economy to one founded on knowledge capture, value-added manufacturing production, and services. In future, the growth in services will easily outstrip growth in resources and manufacturing. Goods production will still increase in absolute dollar terms, but growth will not generally occur in volume production, but value enhancing production. The major challenge as we enter the 21st century will be the revolutionary changes in the mix and characteristics of jobs.

Job losses will **accelerate** in many of our archetypal sectors, but particularly the resource sectors, basic manufacturing and the various levels of the public sector. Jobs will be created in an array of expanding areas such as personal services, tourism, adult education, health care, value added goods production, high technology and knowledge-based services. The problem will be the mismatch of skills and knowledge. Many of the job losses will occur in the reasonably well paid, semi-skilled jobs of the old economy, often operating under the strong union umbrella. The next decade will see the gutting of these "middle jobs." The new jobs will be increasingly polarized at two ends of the spectrum - the low paid, unskilled service jobs and the higher paid, knowledge processing jobs in both the goods and services sectors. The result will be an increasing polarization of society into "haves" and "have nots."

Retraining will be crucial for the unskilled or semi-skilled workers displaced by restructuring. Jobs will be created in the skilled technical areas, as part of our march towards knowledge processing. The failure to retrain, however, will doom the semi-skilled, displaced workers to the poorly paid, unchallenged environment of the more menial service sector jobs. The restructuring means the inevitable decline in union membership and weakening union power.

The Prospect of Real Income Declines

Until recent years it has been our almost unalienable right to expect our real incomes to increase. Certainly until the 1970s, strong economic growth, comprising both a rapidly growing population and labour force, combined with productivity gains continued to propel real incomes. In the 1980s, real incomes for most individuals began to flatten, as productivity lagged (notably in the services sector), but was offset by the catalyst of a rapidly growing labour force of baby-boom entrants and a surge in the female participation rate. This helped maintain Canadian economic growth in the annual 3 percent plus range. The future does not look as rosy, as productivity especially in services continues to lag and labour force growth turns sluggish, as the small baby bust cohort enters the labour force. Together this probably means more sluggish economic growth, nearer 2-2.5 percent annually rather than 3 percent plus, and more significantly the prospect of declining real incomes. This will be exacerbated in an era of more persistently high levels of unemployment yet co-existing with skill shortages. The economic reformation will accentuate the chronic mismatch of skills with shortages in the new economy sectors and surpluses in the old economy sectors. In the failing industries and in the unskilled component of the services sectors, intense competition will place downward pressure on wages and salaries. Real incomes will fall and in many of the "old industries" a two-tier wage system will develop with new hirees being brought on at lower wages.

Meanwhile, in the growing knowledge intensive and value creating sectors there will be shortages of the right skills and knowledge resources. This is an accentuation of elements we see today. Employees with the right mix and blend of technical expertise, commercial smarts, and relational and communication skills will find the job market particularly favourable.

Personal real incomes have in reality been falling for a decade, but this has been masked by a major sociological shift - the large growth in the female participation rate. This has, in fact, lead to slight increases in family income and has given a temporary boost to living standards. This phenomenon is now largely history, as the female participation rate in the prime working age group of 25-44 year-olds now closely approaches that of males. Thus, the future is one that will see falling real family as well as personal incomes for most of the population.

The future will see a large increase in unconventional job patterns, in part driven by a desire to shore up declining real incomes, but also due to radical changes in job markets. As the solid, long term secure job market is eroded in large corporations and the public sector, unconventional job patterns will mushroom. The "job-for-life" philosophy for so long entrenched in large corporations and the public sector is dead. The unofficial employer-employee contract for long term employment in these sectors will whither. There will be job security for very few in the new economy.

More and more employers will turn to flexible employment practices involving part-time workers, job-share, contract and casual workers. This will enable organizations to adjust to rapidly changing economic conditions in a timely and cost effective manner; no more expensive severance packages, pension plans or benefit packages. Large corporations will retain a core of well qualified, flexible knowledge workers, who will be supplemented by satellites of nomadic contractors.

Thus, the work environment will evolve increasingly to one of self reliance. Employees will have to cater to their own benefit packages, health care coverage and pension planning. Combo-jobs will become much more important, as workers attempt to offset declining real incomes through unconventional work patterns.

Declining real incomes will increase the need for moonlighting. This will be exacerbated by rising taxation which will lead to growth in the bartering of services and a swelling of the "underground" economy. The measures of economic activity through conventional real domestic product already understate the true level of economic activity. More work will be hidden behind unincorporated and incorporated business umbrellas to minimize tax payments and maximize expense deductions. Governments will be confronted by a declining tax base as expense and other tax deduction mechanisms such as RRSPs escalate at unprecedented rates.

The reduction in the real tax base will reinforce the contraction in the social safety net, which, in turn, exacerbates the social polarization of society.

Moonlighting will become the growth industry of the 21st century. The "need" to offset declining real incomes, avoid onerous taxation and the lack of full time, secure jobs will lead to a more entrepreneurial, opportunistic underground economy. Increasingly the home will become a denizen of business activity for both home-based business and telecommuting. The development of communications technology combined with low cost will curtail growth in commercial developments, especially in crowded and congested downtown environments. This will exacerbate vacant office space in the metropolitan core as more home-based businesses are developed and telecommuting leads to both productivity gains and cost savings (for example, shared office space).

The municipal revenue base will decline as office space in the core metropolitan areas contract, and migration of more business to the home does not compensate with commensurate tax revenues.

The Job Market

As a parent of two young adults, it is not difficult to see that the job market of the 1990s has changed. When I emigrated from England to Canada in 1970, the last thing on my mind as a well qualified mineral explorationist was whether I would get a job. It was more a matter of choice; which job on which continent.

Yet today, well qualified engineers, scientists, teachers, nurses, lawyers and others often find themselves without job prospects in their field. This book has discussed many of the reasons for the frustrations felt by many young people. The economic transformation has hollowed out almost all large corporations and curtailed growth in our large public sector. Furthermore, many of Canada's staple industries and corporations have entered the life cycle stage of maturity or in many cases senility. Employees caught in these industries, irrespective of knowledge and skills, have become casualties of the economic reformation. In some cases competencies are readily transferred to the new growth engines, but in many cases transference is inhibited by the specificity of the competency suite. The future portends more of the same, as large corporations continue to downsize and the public sector becomes the focus for the same squeeze in the mid-to-late 1990s.

Demographic trends are also exerting intense pressure on employment trends. The large cohort of baby-boomers are being squeezed down market, "stealing" many of the starter jobs that would normally be open to the baby busters entering the work force. In turn, intense competitive pressures in virtually all markets compel organizations and businesses to choose experience, if possible, over rookie job entrants. In a world of contracting large organizations and the downward squeeze of the big cohort baby-boomers it is not surprising that the new entrant baby-busters are being forced into the secondary satellite market of part-time or contract labour or out of their field of specialization completely.

What most observers fail to recognize is that the job market has been revolutionized. What worked in our day is now of little relevance. The "safe" jobs of old are in many cases the fossils of the future. In their wake, restructuring and technology has given birth to a whole suite of new jobs. Many of these literally did not exist in the 1970s. In many cases these new age jobs are in the para-professional ranks - these are the jobs that will propel us into the 21st century.

What are the general competencies required in today's job market? Well first of all competencies have two components - knowledge and skills. To some extent these two words can be used as synonyms for education and training. This immediately brings us to one of the most controversial debates raging in modern society - the role of education facilities versus the demands of the workplace. Educators argue, rightfully I believe, that the role of schools and academic post-secondary institutions is education in a broader sense. They believe their role is a somewhat loftier one to produce well rounded, responsible citizens for Canadian society. Providing education and specific skills for the workplace, however, should be a major component of this objective, but not necessarily the exclusive one. Vocational institutions, on the other hand, unabashedly exist to provide direct knowledge and particularly skills for the workplace.

This is becoming one of the biggest dilemmas of modern Canadian society, particularly as we enter a new era of hostile international competition and a slowdown in economic growth. The major question becomes how much do we change our fundamental school and university systems to become more vocationally-oriented? Rightly or wrongly the economic czars in our society will be increasing that pressure.

Today, the complete competency suite is a triumvirate of three components - a technical function, a commercial function and a relational function. This is broadly true today for the spectrum of jobs from the executive suite to the factory floor to the counter worker. Thus, the new entrant, and indeed present incumbents, are under strong pressure today to develop a broader set of competencies, beyond their specific technical abilities.

Thus, for most workers there is a requirement to develop a broad foundation of skills embracing a specific technical expertise, some commercial smarts, good oral and written communication skills, inter-personal relationship skills, networking abilities and fundamental computer literacy. Upon this foundation, most of us will be expected to develop specialty peaks. These specialty peaks will evolve over time and each peak may have a time span of 4-6 years. In most of the workplace, workers will not only have many jobs in a lifetime, but several different careers. This is a world of lifelong learning and continuous upgrading of our competency suite.

By way of example, let us take a professional engineer joining a large chemical company. The engineer starts life as a process engineer in a plastics resin plant, before moving into an environmental position and then follows a career path encompassing public affairs, human resource management, information technology and financial ventures. Moreover, these different careers are more likely to occur in different organizations, rather than the one organization. This is symptomatic of the future workplace.

Constant changes in the work environment and a more holistic approach to training will mean the development of the education continuum. Conventional learning in school to the age of 18 will become only a small component of a lifelong learning process. This is not professional elitism, as this will apply also to the ranks of para-professionals, technicians, trades and semi-skilled workers. The role of computers and telecommunications will become pervasive at all echelons of society. The trucking industry, for instance, already uses satellite communications technology for fleet management optimization. The future will bring on-board guidance systems for route optimization, involving the acquisition of new skills. Many of the conventional trades are experiencing significant changes, involving substantial retraining. Much of the pipeline welding is being automated. The car mechanic faces a plethora of change as automobiles acquire computers, anti-lock braking systems, new types of suspensions systems, new types of materials, turbochargers and in the near future automated guidance systems, new drive trains and maybe non-cooled ceramic engines.

The future will entail a much greater commitment to training at all levels. Increasingly, the financing of this education will move from the public to private domain. Organizational budgets for training and re-education will rise significantly, but also more of the cost burden will be borne by the individual. Increasingly new private institutions geared to work-related skills will encroach upon the prevailing dominance of public institutions. Continued funding constraints and in many cases lack of vision or desire to move to more vocationally-oriented education will lead to a contraction of many post-secondary institutions.

Jobs of the Future

In the job market beware - the past is a poor indicator of the future. Failure to take into account the transformation of our economy, technological change, demographic trends and our changing global competitiveness leads most observers and career counselors to take a very static view of the job market. But, the job market is being revolutionized with many of our base-load jobs fading into oblivion and a whole set of new jobs rising in their wake.

Let's just set the scene on the theme of this book. The economic reformation suggests a decline in most resource-based industries and, at best, stagnation in many basic manufacturing industries. Instead, we see growth in value creation processing, niche manufacturer markets, a growth in small business, services and new technology-intensive businesses. In a microcosm, this means a requirement for fewer geologists, forestry scientists, farmers, fishermen, reservoir engineers, off-highway truck drivers and mining engineers. Yet, on the positive side a whole new dimension of growth for professionals and skilled technicians in telecommunications, lasers, computer assisted manufacturing and design, biotechnology, polymer chemistry, catalyst chemistry, robotics, the tourist industry, health care, adult education instruction, personal services, and the export of our natural resources and infrastructure expertise globally.

It is this dichotomy in job opportunities that is setting the stage for the most pressing issue of the 21st century - the grave mismatch of skills. The more we look back to the old economy, the more people that will be doomed to the job scrap heap. On the other hand, those with foresight will enter the new emerging fields with bright futures, and good job prospects, albeit with less security and stability than in the past. Over the years, I have had the opportunity of presenting my views on job trends to many diverse audiences in the vocational and adult retraining area. It is indeed tragic that in many areas the advice and counseling given to the younger generation is pitifully inadequate and blissfully ignorant of fundamental economic change. In particular, the counseling services in our high school systems is in a total time warp. They are preparing children for 1970s careers, which are at best stagnant and in many cases already in rapid decline.

The job market trends that I will discuss in this section are literally a fall out of the previous sections of the book. They are a pure outcome of the earlier elucidated trends. But, the main message is that the job market as we enter the 21st century is very different from the job market of the last twenty years. Ignore this fact at your peril.

The Future Job Scene

Getting the right competency mix is the key for future employability. If in doubt stack the deck with too many rather than too few. But, make sure they are the right competencies.

It will be particularly important to understand the difference between knowledge and skills. It is ironic that in a future-economy that focuses on knowledge-intensity, that many knowledge-intensive workers are unemployed or unemployable. Looking at it solely from a vocational perspective, one must be very specific on what knowledge is needed in the new economy and critically what is the balance of knowledge and skills in specific jobs.

In many areas of the economy, outside of the true professional ranks, skills rank higher than knowledge. Let me elaborate with a simple example of the ubiquitous computer. Computer experts in programming, architecture and computer hardware design need in-depth knowledge on the physics and engineering of computers. To most computer users this is superfluous and irrelevant (except in an academic sense of being better educated). Most of us computer hacks need the skills to use the myriad software programs for word processing, spreadsheets, graphics, database management and electronic files. It is these latter skills that are more useful for most employees in the global workplace, rather than a knowledge of computer hardware itself.

The knowledge to skills ratio (KSR) will become the key ingredient for employability. This will determine placement within the job hierarchy of society. There are basically four levels of jobs within the Canadian job market.

1. Those with a high knowledge to skills ratio - usually designated as PROFESSIONALS
2. Those with a balanced knowledge to skills ratio - what I will call PARA-PROFESSIONALS or TECHNICIANS
3. Those with a high skills to knowledge ratio - what I will call the TRADES or PARA-TECHNICIANS
4. Those with a low skill/low knowledge base - the UNSKILLED.

Understanding where jobs fit is crucial to developing the right competency mix. Beyond that comes the decision of acquiring the right knowledge and the right skills. Knowledge per se is no true salvation for job security - it is only knowledge that is valued by the workplace that offers job security. All university degrees are knowledge-intensive, but not all have knowledge relevant to gaining employment. Likewise it is important to acquire future oriented skills rather than skills prone to redundancy.

The new economy will bring a different emphasis to the job market and vastly different job growth patterns than the past. Among the professional ranks it is critical to understand future job trends. A university education is no longer a guarantee for premium employment opportunities; hence the many PH.Ds driving taxis today. Understanding the value of specific professions in the new economy is critical.

One of the largest growth areas in the future economy will be in the ranks of the para-professional and the technicians. This is, in part, in response to extreme cost pressures, but also a subtle shift in many areas of our economy from knowledge to skills. It also involves a more critical evaluation of jobs and the over-employment of professionals in areas quite capable of being as well served by less qualified and less expensive workers. The next decade will in many respects belong to the para-professional and skilled technician, drawn from the ranks of institutions unequivocally geared to vocational training.

The Professional Job Market

The paradigm that I have painted of value creation, knowledge intensity and high technology is a positive environment for many professional jobs, but certainly not all. The sector as a whole will continue to grow, but subdividing this diverse market reveals a set of very contrasting trends. Many resources-based professions will inevitably decline in the mining, fishing, agricultural, forestry and oil industries. Many of these professions are also "functionally restrictive" as they are geared very specifically to one industry and have poor transferable skills. A geologist is basically married to the oil and gas and mining industries - unlike more generic professions such as accounting and law, the skill set is not readily transferable to other growth-oriented businesses and sectors. These are the real "danger" professions - narrow, specialized and sector specific. In many cases these are the professions I call the laggards (see Appendix). This is not to say jobs will not continue to exist, but they are in a declining market and in intensely competitive, waning industries, exercising extreme cost consciousness and, in most cases, ongoing contraction.

Many professionals fall in a category that I call the mainstays. They are not, in general, declining, but, on the other hand, they are not professions that will expand their ranks rapidly. Accountants, lawyers, mainstream engineers, doctors and dentists are in this category, but with one caveat. Cost pressures in a more sluggish, economic future will put much more pressure on professional services and undoubtedly, as we enter the next century I see a strong increase in the para-professional ranks. This will be driven by continuing cost reductions in the public sector, as well as a more pressing cost control by individuals in an environment of declining real family incomes. Overall, there will be a trend to extracting more value from professionals and the winnowing of more routinized functions to lower cost para-professionals and skilled technicians.

The real rising stars in the professional ranks are geared to the newly emerging businesses in a restructured Canadian economy such as value-added manufacturing, high technology, the environment, health care, adult education, design, tourism, personal services, and marketing our natural resources and telecommunications expertise overseas.

The Coming Boom in Para-professionals and Technicians

We are entering an age of the more discerning consumer, and increasing cost pressures in both the private and public sectors. Life cycle analysis suggests that like many advanced industrialized nations our economy has passed its peak. Future economic growth will probably be slower than we have experienced in the last twenty years. This is probably part and parcel of the maturation of advanced industrial societies generally, as emerging nations in Asia and Latin America become the global engines of growth. Undoubtedly, the maturation theory also becomes intertwined with sustainability issues. More environmental consciousness and a re-evaluation of lifestyles and values will also probably push us into an era of more constrained growth.

In this environment, real family incomes will likely fall. Government debts at all levels, federal, provincial and municipal, must be approaching their zenith. The pressure for future governments, independent of ideological hue, to balance their budgets will be intense, both from the international finance community and the electorate. The Canadian public is rapidly realizing there is not such thing as a free lunch.

In a nutshell, the future is about controlling costs and seeking more economic alternatives and better value for money. For governments it means looking at delivering critical services such as education and health care cheaper. For the individual consumer it means stretching the dollar further and reducing costs. No environment is more favorable for the emergence of the para-professional or skilled technician. In many instances, substantial cost savings can be realized at little or no sacrifice of quality.

Para-professionals and skilled technicians will be the job wave of the future. Many of the functions now carried out by higher paid professionals will be practiced by para-professionals. This will be driven by the desire of private and public sector organizations to reduce costs, as well as reducing consumer expenditures in an era of contracting real incomes. Para-legals, teaching assistants, nursing practitioners, dental hygienists, midwives, police ancillaries, para-accountants and engineering technologists will flourish as the focus on cost containment and value for money intensifies.

The word "para" originates from the Greek word and in a literal sense means beside. These para-professionals will indeed co-exist alongside the professionals, although they will hardly be warmly received by their professional counterparts. Para-professionals will intensify competition among many professions, eroding their fee structures and professional monopolies and reducing the need for their services.

In turn, many of the new technology drivers are a boon for skilled technicians, particularly in the new manufacturing economy. Automation has eroded many of the semi-skilled jobs in basic manufacturing, but in its wake has emerged a whole suite of new jobs for skilled technology. Automation is less a destroyer of jobs than it is a re-designer of skill-sets. As an example, the new world of information technology, robotics and automation has created new high skill requirements for robotic maintenance personnel, computer assisted manufacturing and design technicians, laser technicians, electronics technicians, instrumentation technologists and materials technologists.

The Trades and Para-Technicians

The role of many of the skilled tradesperson and para-technician in our future economy has been substantially neglected. In the futurist's quest to convey the need for knowledge intensity and value-adding goods and services, the role of the trades somehow evaporates or is neglected.

While certain trades are very amenable to automation and hence the number of trades people required will be less, many trades are certainly not substitutable by machines in the foreseeable future. Indeed, with increasing time pressures in society more demands will be placed on many trades. Also favouring trades opportunities is a pervasive societal move for many people to aspire at advanced academic training for their children. An academic snobbishness is being cultivated, resulting in a surfeit of new professional graduates, but a deficit in certain trades.

Certainly, increasing automation and new equipment will quell our appetite for some trades such as welding, automobile mechanics, carpentry and painting. Most trades, however, are not readily amenable to automation in the near future. One only has to think of the plumber and electrician and it is highly unlikely that robotics in the near future will make a dent on their workload. It would certainly be quite a robot capable of wiring a house or office building. The future economy will certainly change the type of work for many trades, with much more emphasis on retrofitting and renovations rather than new construction. Also shifting tastes and values will lead to a resurgence in demand for many trades such as bricklayers and stonemasons and finishing craft carpenters. Roofers specializing in tile will outstrip growth of roofers for other materials. Despite our evolution to a knowledge-based economy, there will remain a very healthy demand for many trades.

APPENDIX

JOB TRENDS IN CANADA

JOB TRENDS - PROFESSIONAL

LAGGARDS	MAINSTAYS	RISING STARS
Architects	Accountants	Actors/Actresses
Aeronautical Engineers	Agricultural Scientists	Adult Educators
Agricultural Engineers	Buyers	Agricultural Biotechnologists
Biologists	Chemical Engineers	Art/Antique Dealers
Cartographers	Chemists	CAM/CAD Engineers
Clergy	Civil Engineers	Commercial Artists
Corporate Planners	Doctors	Computer Programmers
Dentists	Firefighters	Computer Software Writers
Forestry Scientists	Food/Hygiene Inspectors	Data Management
Geologists	Funeral Directors	Consultants
Health Care Administrators	Health Counsellors	Dieticians
Marine Surveyors	Insurance Agents	EDI Consultants
Metallurgists	Lawyers	Electronic Engineers
Microbiologists	Librarians	Energy Management
Middle Management	Market Research Professionals	Consultants
Military Officers	Mathematicians	Environmental Scientists
Mining Engineers	Mechanical Engineers	Expert Systems Consultants
Nuclear Scientists	Optometrists	Financial Advisors
Park Wardens	Photographers	Geriatric Consultants
Petroleum Engineers	Pilots	Health/Fitness Professionals
Physicists	Police Officers	Helicopter Pilots
Public Relations Specialists	Sales Managers	Industrial Hygienists
Oceanographers	Social welfare Officers	Industrial Designers
Research Professionals	Speech Therapists	Information Mgmt. Specialists
Reservoir Engineers	Teachers	Information Systems
School Administrators	Urban Planners	Librarians
Surveyors	Veterinarians	Information Security Advisors
University Professors		Linguistic Specialists
Zoologists		Marketers
		Materials Engineers
		Nurses
		Office Electronic Specialists
		Orthodontists
		Pharmacists
		Plastic/Cosmetic Surgeons
		Productivity Consultants
		Psychologists
		Quality Control Consultants
		Rehabilitation Counsellors
		Robot Designers
		Robot Programmers
		Telemarketing Specialists
		Telecommunications
		Specialists
		Travel Consultants
		Vocational Advisors
		Waste Treatment Engineers
		Workplace Consultants

JOB TRENDS - PARA-PROFESSIONAL/TECHNOLOGISTS

LAGGARDS	MAINSTAYS	RISING STARS
Conventional Design Artists (non-computer) Farmers Fishermen Machine Operators Military Personnel Receptionists Secretaries Typists	Air Traffic Controllers Carpet Weavers Chemical Technicians Florists Horticulturalists Laboratory Technicians Machinists Real Estate Agents Sawmill Operators	Broadcast Media Technicians CAM Mechanics CAM/CAD Technologists CAM Production Scheduler Chefs Computer Drafting and Graphics Technicians Dental Hygienists Dental Laboratory Technicians Electronic Technologists Energy Conservation Technicians Laser Technicians Lifeguards Midwives Nursing Practitioners Paralegals Paramedics Parapolice Recycling Specialists Robotic Technologists Security Business Specialists Telephone/Cable Installers Travel Agents

JOB TRENDS - TRADES

LAGGARDS	MAINSTAYS	RISING STARS
Agricultural Mechanics Boatbuilders Cabinet Makers Cement Finishers Crane and Hoisting Operators Engineering Draftspersons Glaziers Industrial Painters Insulators Ironworkers Jewellers Metal cutters Millwrights Paper Mill Operators Pulp Mill Operators Printing Press Operators Refrigeration Mechanics Roofers (asphalt/shingles) Sheet Metal Mechanics Steel Fabricators Textile Machine Operators Tool/Die Makers Typesetters Welders	Aircraft Mechanics Appliance Service Engineers Bartenders Blacksmiths Boilermakers Chemical Operators Diesel Mechanics Electricians Gasfitters Heavy Duty Mechanics Machinists Motor Mechanics Motorcycle Mechanics Plasterers Plumbers Pipefitters Power Linemen Tilesetters Upholsterers	Autobody Mechanics Bakers Beauticians/Cosmetologists Bricklayers/Stonemasons Carpenters Cooks Hairdressers Instrument Mechanics Landscape Architects Masseurs Painters/Decorators Recreation Vehicle Mechanics Roofers (tile) Sprinkler Systems Installers

JOB TRENDS - OTHER

LAGGARDS	MAINSTAYS	RISING STARS
Assemblers - Production Line	Bus Drivers	Crafts Specialists
Cashiers	Correctional Institutional	Day Care Workers
Counter Clerks	Officers	Food Counter Workers
Drilling Rig Operators	Fork Lift Operators	Housecleaners
Farm Labourers	Hotel/Motel Clerks	Locksmiths
File Clerks	Retail Sales Workers	Nannies
Freight Handlers	Sanitary Engineers	Pet Care Workers
Inventory Clerks	Truck Drivers	Renovation Contractors
Keypunch Operators		Waiters/Waitresses
Loggers		
Materials Handlers		
Meter Readers		
Municipal Workers		
Postal Workers		
Service Station Attendants		
Shipping/Receiving Clerks		
Switchboard Operators		
Tailors		
Telephone Operators		
Train Drivers		

NOTES

NOTES

ORDER FORM

Give the Perfect Gift to a Friend!

Please send _____ copies of

BUSINESS TRENDS KALEIDOSCOPE

by

Roger J. Goodman

to

Name _____

Address _____

_____

_____

Postal Code _____

Forward cheque or money order for $14.95 per book
(plus $2.00 per book for postage and handling)
payable to

KERNOW ENTERPRISES INC.

818 Varsity Estates Place
Calgary, Alberta
T3B 3X3

Please contact Kernow Enterprises Inc. for quotations on large orders.